FOLKLORE

OF

ANCIENT WILTSHIRE

The original version of this work was prepared and submitted as a Master's dissertation; as such it was annotated with scrupulous references to source documents. When the decision to publish was taken, it was felt that such a large number of references would be obtrusive and of little interest to the general reader. Therefore I have kept footnotes to a minimum, using them only to identify quotations and to acknowledge supporting evidence and comments by folklore writers. The sources of the folklore itself, together with the other works of interest, will be found in the comprehensive bibliography at the end of the book.

Ornance Survey map references have been included for the convenience of those who wish to locate or visit the sites.

Cover picture: The Devil's Den near Marlborough

FOLKLORE

OF

ANCIENT WILTSHIRE

KATHARINE M. JORDAN

WILTSHIRE COUNTY COUNCIL, LIBRARY & MUSEUM SERVICE

1990

Published by
Wiltshire County Council, Library & Museum Service, Bythesea Road, Trowbridge, Wiltshire, BA14 8BS.

Director R. L. Pybus, MA, FLA, FCIS, MILAM, MBIM.

1990

I.S.B.N. 0 86080 194 2

CONTENTS

MAPS AND ILLUSTRATIONS

LIST OF PHOTOGRAPHS

INTRODUCTION

"The business of the folklorist is to trace the growth and diffusion of tradition, possibly to advance theories of its origin or to examine those already put forward,"[1]

This statement by Briggs puts into perspective a basic problem faced by any student of folklore: how to tell whether a 'tradition' dates from early times or just from last century. Interpretation of customs and legends is fascinating, but fraught with dangers for the unwary. One is liable to find that the seemingly ancient pagan fertility rite performed at "Sprockton Parva" every May Day was actually instituted on the whim of a nineteenth-century rector with a taste for the picturesque. The fact that such customs and legends are transmitted orally adds to the confusion, as each new generation adapts and innovates, until the original purpose is almost obscured by time and the ebb and flow of ideas.

Fortunately for the amateur, the origin of traditions, as Briggs makes clear, is not of primary importance. Rather it is the types of lore and legend which can be shown to exist, or to have existed, their growth and distribution, and how they express the ideas and attitudes of the local people, which is of most interest to the folklorist.

The study of traditions connected with Prehistoric and Dark Age sites would seem to be a rather neglected branch of folklore. Apart from the seminal works by L. V. Grinsell, there has been little regional study carried out specifically in this area. It is an ideal subject for local research.

This study attempts first and foremost to bring together some of the written accounts of such folklore in Wiltshire, and to show how they conform to themes which occur throughout the country at ancient sites. These themes are considered generally in Chapter I, which presents the background archaeology and folklore against which the subsequent illustrative chapters are set. The secondary aim of the study is to offer some (fairly guarded) criticism and interpretation of the folklore encountered. Wherever possible this has been based on the authority of experts, and otherwise on historical, topographical and etymological evidence, leavened with common sense.

[1] K. M. Briggs, *A dictionary of fairies* (Harmondsworth, 1977), p. xvi

FACT AND FOLKLORE

"They heard of the Great Barrows, and the green mounds, and the stone-rings upon the hills and in the hollows among the hills ... Green walls and white walls rose. There were fortresses on the heights. Kings of little kingdoms fought together, and the young Sun shone like fire upon the red metal of their new and greedy swords. There was victory and defeat; and towers fell, fortresses were burned, and flames went up into the sky. Gold was piled on the biers of dead kings and queens; and mounds covered them, and the stone doors were shut; and the grass grew over all. Sheep walked for a while biting the grass, but soon the hills were empty again. A shadow came out of dark places far away, and the bones were stirred in the mounds... Stone-rings grinned out of the ground like broken teeth in the moonlight".[1]

The taste for the mysterious and unknown which is such a feature of the human character, has long found expression in the weaving of strange tales about ancient places. Unable to interpret the long-forsaken (and therefore mysterious) mounds and earthworks as modern archaeological methods allow contemporary man to do, our ancestors still were not at a loss, but exercised their imaginations, so giving rise to the curious and often wildy bizarre legends which surround ancient sites. It is with such tales and traditions that this study is chiefly concerned, but before considering these 'shadows' which come out of the 'dark places' of man's imaginations it seems appropriate to look briefly, in the light of modern archaeology, at the origins and purpose of 'the Great Barrows, and the green mounds, and the stone-rings'.

4000	3000	2000	1000	BC	AD
Neolithic		Earlier	Later	Iron Age	
		Bronze Age			
Long barrows					
Enclosures					
Henge monuments		......			
Round barrows					
Stone circles					
Hill-forts					
Land boundaries				......	

Different types of site and the general periods when they are reckoned to have been constructed. (*after* N. Thomas)

[1] J. R. R. Tolkien, *The Fellowship of the Ring*, 2nd ed. (London, 1966), p. 141.

Long barrows are specialised tombs in which the communal burial of members of a tribe would have taken place. The earliest long barrows are simple earthen mounds, but the later megalithic ('big stone') chamber tombs were built with massive undressed boulders. Chamber tombs are of two types: passage graves, rare in Britain, in which a passage leads to a main chamber; and gallery graves, such as the West Kennet long barrow, in which a parallel-sided passage opens onto side chambers. Related structures are dolmens or cromlechs, simple chambers, often found minus their earthen mounds, comprising a capstone resting usually on three uprights.

The earthworks known as **causewayed camps**, or **interrupted ditch enclosures**, are, as the alternative name suggests, enclosures bounded by a single ditch or several concentric ditches dug in sections broken by causewayed entrances. The enclosures are sometimes found in apparently defensive positions such as hilltops and spurs, but are also found on level ground or beside rivers. They were once thought to be settlements, hence the name 'camp', but latterly such writers as N. Thomas express the view, based on archaeological evidence, that "most causewayed camps served as fairs, or rallying points, where Neolithic farmers foregathered at certain times of the year for social contact, for barter, for exchange of ideas and perhaps for worship".[2] It is notable that the use of enclosures for fairs continued well into the last century.

Henge monuments appear to have originated in Britain during the third millennium BC. They are roughly circular areas bounded by a ditch with a bank outside it, broken usually by one or two entrance gaps. These sacred sites lie normally on low ground, often near water, as do both Avebury and Stonehenge, the two such monuments dealt with here. Henges take their name from Stonehenge: the word means 'hanging' and derives from the Stonehenge doorway-like trilithons, stones which hang in the air. However, the word has come to mean the type of enclosure formed in the first phase of Stonehenge's construction, rather than any standing stone associated with the earthwork.

Standing stones or **monoliths** are of two types: those shaped by man, and those naturally shaped by geological action and the weather. Sarsen stone, an extremely hard sandstone rock, occurs naturally upon the chalk downs of Wiltshire, and so was used by ancient peoples in building tombs, the Avebury complex, and the great trilithons of Stonehenge.

The Bronze Age saw the completed transition from the communal to solitary burial. **Round barrows** were erected principally over a single

[2] N. Thomas, *Guide to Prehistoric England,* (London, 1976), p. 14.

corpse, although secondary burials might be placed at the sides of the mound at a later date. The types of round barrow are many, but four main variants can be discerned. The bell-barrow is a large mound separated from a surrounding ditch, and possibly bank too, by a flat space or 'berm'. Two or three mounds might be surrounded by one ditch. Bell-barrows often covered male interments. Females were placed beneth disc-barrows, small mounds separated from ditch and bank by a wide berm. Again, two or three mounds could be bounded by one ditch. Saucer-barrows more often covered female interments, while the most common bowl-barrows, simple mounds surrounded by a ditch and perhaps a bank, covered burials of either sex. Burial was either by cremation, or inhumation of the skeleton fully clothed, with appropriate grave goods, the flesh having been allowed to decay beforehand.

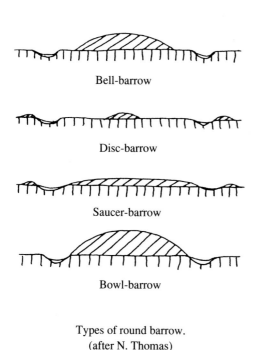

Bell-barrow

Disc-barrow

Saucer-barrow

Bowl-barrow

Types of round barrow.
(after N. Thomas)

The Iron Age saw the construction of **hill-forts** in great numbers, mainly on high ground although some occur on flat low ground which affords a good all-round view. Most early forts comprise a single uninterrupted bank and ditch, while later earthworks form multivallate enclosures. Often hill-forts overlie earlier Neolithic causewayed camps. They might have served simply as stock corrals, or as ramparted villages forming the focus for one community.

Linear earthworks which are apparently boundaries between the territories of different tribes, are found widely throughout the southern parts of Britain. Of the two such sites considered here, Grim's Ditch is the older, thought to be of Bronze Age date, while Wansdyke, which cuts across a Roman road, is therefore believed to date, like Offa's Dyke, from the Dark Ages.

So much for the archaeological evidence of the ways of our ancestors. Folklore can offer a different kind of evidence, at once less reliable, because it has been blurred and adapted over many years, and more immediate, because the essential spirit of the lore has remained, a living thing still enclosed within the trappings of past centuries.

Many traditions have grown up from the interaction between **paganism and Christianity**. As Aubrey Burl explains: "The Christian Church did not weed out paganism. It came to terms with it and the two grew together, intertwined, so that some of our most ancient past is still with us."[3] This toleration was deliberate Vatican policy, and Bede records how in AD 601 Pope Gregory I charged Abbot Mellitus, and through him St. Augustine, not to destroy pagan sacred sites, but rather to take them over for Christian worship, so that the new converts might not be confronted with too direct a conflict of loyalties, but might continue worshipping in their accustomed places.[4] Some evidence of this policy remains in the careful siting of some ancient churches beside standing stones, tumuli and henges. At Knowlton, Dorset, the ruins of a Norman church stand within one of a line of three henges; while in Wiltshire, though no churches are set within henges or hill-forts, the church at Avebury stands close beside the henge and stone circle. The intent behind such sitings must surely have been to insist upon Christianity's supremacy over paganism. Similarly, the Church spread tales, like that of the blacksmith St. Dunstan pinching the Devil's nose with pincers, which illustrated the victory of Christianity over paganism.

The ranks of the **Saints** were called upon to aid the smooth takeover of power. As K. Thomas has said: "the ancient worship of wells, trees and stones was not so much abolished as modified, by turning pagan sites into Christian ones and associating them with a saint rather than a heathen deity".[5] For instance, St. Bride or Brigid was an Irish saint said to be midwife to the Virgin, and patron saint of childbirth. Her cult closely resembled that of the Celtic fertility goddess Brigantia, to whom women made offerings at springs and wells in the hope that they would bear children, and it seems almost certain that the many Brideswells and Brigid's wells that exist in many parts of Britain were once sacred to Brigantia.

Pagan festivals were absorbed into the church year. The yule log and mistletoe took their place in the trappings of Christmas, though it is notable that mistletoe was never permitted in church. The Celtic quarter days Imbolc, Lugnasad and Samhain became Candlemas (February 1st), Lammas (August 1st), and All Saints Day (November 1st) respectively, though the

[3] A. Burl, *Prehistoric Avebury*, (London, 1979), p. 27
[4] Bede, *Ecclesiastical history of the English nation*, (London, 1910) pp. 52-3.
[5] K. Thomas, *Religion and the decline of magic*, (London, 1971), pp. 47-8.

darker side of Samhain lingers in Hallowe'en. Beltane (May 1st) has continued as a day of semi-pagan festival, marked by dancing about the phallic maypole, and by ancient death and rebirth mimes performed by a hobby horse and his attendants.

As a general rule, the god of one religion turns into the Devil of the religion which replaces it; and so the **Devil** has come to be much associated with ancient sites, especially those of religious significance. The number of Devil names, such as 'Devil's Quoits' or 'Devil's Den', may bear witness to attempts by the church to prevent its errant flock from going to pagan stones to worship or work magic. Another aspect of Devil-lore is the fiend's role in the legendary creation of hills, both natural and manmade. Often there is a colourful legend telling how Satan intended to bury some town with a huge clod of earth, but was prevented from doing so by quick thinking on the part of a mortal. The 'clod of earth' remains as a hill to testify to the defeat of the Devil by a person of faith.

Similar to the Devil is **Grim**, a personage widely associated with linear earthworks. Many Grimsdykes are also known as Devil's dykes. Grim or Grimnir was one of the by-names of **Woden** or Odin, the Allfather of the Norse pantheon. The name signifies one hooded or masked, and refers to the god's habit of appearing in disguise. Margaret Gelling suggests that place-names containing the element 'Woden' represents areas where paganism lingered after the general acceptance of Christianity[6], while B. Branston goes one step further. Noting the number of 'Woden' names in and around the Vale of Pewsey, he suggests that this indicates that the area was a centre for the worship of Woden, who would thus have been the obvious candidate for constructing vast linear earthworks or barrows. Woden was worshipped in Saxon Wessex and Essex, Anglian Mercia, and Jutish Kent, and some of their royal houses traced their descent from him. There were two aspects to Woden's character as he was worshipped in Britain. He was the divine magician whose self-sacrifice had brought wisdom to men: hence he was invoked in spells, ornamented genealogies and was believed to have created great earthworks. But he was also a wind and sky god with power over the dead, leading his Wild Hunt across the sky in pursuit of souls, particularly those of hanged men, for the traditional form of sacrifice to Woden was by hanging. "The Anglo-Saxon Woden stalked the rolling downland, one-eyed and wise beyond all knowing in cloak and hood when the weather was fine, stopping at cross-roads to recognise his own dangling from the gallows; but on black and stormy nights he racketed across the sky at the head of his wild hunt of lost and stormy souls."[7]

[6] M. Gelling, *Signposts to the past*, (London, 1978), p. 158.
[7] B. Branston, *The lost gods of England*, (London, 1974), pp. 4, 107.

Various kinds of legendary and supernatural beings besides gods and demons are recalled in folklore of ancient sites. Round barrows are sometimes said to be fairy hills, from which occasionally comes fairy music. The earliest **fairies** were of human size, like Thomas of Ercildoune's "ladye bright" who took him to Elfland, but by the seventeenth century they had dwindled into the little people we think of today, dwelling in woods and fairy hills, dancing in fairy rings, and having a complicated social structure of their own. The name 'fairy' is thought to be derived from the classical three Fates who multipled over the years to become the Fays, supernatural women who directed human destiny and attended childbirths. 'Fay-erie' at first signified a state of enchantment, but later came to mean the fays who possessed the power to enchant. The origins of the fairies themselves, as distinct from the derivation of the name, are still obscure. The expert Kathleen Briggs notes three main theories: that fairies are dwindled gods or nature spirits; that they are the memory of a more primitive race driven into hiding by later invaders; and that they are the souls of the dead, waiting to rejoin their bodies on the day of judgement. However, Briggs stresses that folklorists are interested not so much in the origins of fairy beliefs, as in whether their existence is believed in by those who tell about them.[8]

While fairies dwindled in size, some of the **Giants** grew from ordinary human size to giant proportions. Folk heroes have a habit of growing in size as their reputations grow. Other giants were once gods, like Bran the Blessed in the Welsh myths. They vary in intelligence and malice, for some are gentle and foolish, while others, such as the ogre killed by Jack in the nursery tale, are cruel and bloodthirsty. Giants share with the Devil in folklore the credit for creating natural features of the landscape, and, like the Devil, are often tricked by the cunning of humans. Such remarkable beings were the obvious choice for explaining away the huge long barrows. Who apart from a giant would need so large a grave?

Ghosts are as ubiquitous as they are mysterious. The various scientific explanations of ghosts, for example that they are hallucinations or some kind of spontaneous moving picture replayed from time to time, seem to many no more convincing than the traditional view of them as spirits of the dead, or as elementals. Ghosts do not apparently discriminate between the old and the new in choosing their haunts: there are many reports of ghosts in modern flats and council houses; and even of ghostly cars and lorries. Yet any site steeped in history must be prime territory for ghost-hunting, and ancient sites attract appropriate ghosts. These phantoms tend to be of antique appearance if human, being horsemen or priests; while there are a fair number of animal ghosts, notably large hounds. The **black dog** is a widespread phantom,

[8] K. M. Briggs, *A dictionary of fairies*, (Harmondsworth, 1977), pp. 131, 393-4.

always associated with a definite place or stretch of road. Unlike its baleful cousins the Barguest, Padfoot or Shuck, it does not change its shape or attempt to show the beholder that it is not a normal dog. Yet because it is 'as big as a calf', with 'eyes like burning coals' or 'as big as saucers', anyone seeing it is left in no doubt that they are in the presence of something uncanny. Theo Brown notes that black dogs haunting Prehistoric remains are an important class, and that this association with pre-history together with the persistence of the ghost suggest an archetypal origin.[9] Some have seen the black dog as one of the hounds from the Wild Hunt, and certainly the fact that some hounds, particularly in Wiltshire, drag a chain, recalls Fenrir the fettered wolf of Norse mythology, whose escape is to herald the end of the world. Yet black dog traditions are found in Ireland and Brittany where the Huntsman Odin was never worshipped. Like ghosts everywhere, this phantom keeps its secret.

Various **heroes and villains**, mythological and historical, are recalled in the names and traditions attached to certain ancient sites. Ellis Davidson stresses that folklore heroes are those who have moved over a large area and whose actions have affected many, so that they are adopted by the people as a whole.[10] Typical are the legends of King Arthur and his knights which were popularised both in folk tradition and in the romances of mediaeval writers, so that Arthurian sites occur all over England. However, in Wiltshire it is the activities of Merlin the enchanter which are remembered in folklore. To find Arthur one must go east to Winchester or west to Cadbury Castle. From a later tradition comes Robin Hood, who, whether he existed or not, ranged widely in legend throughout the Midlands and Yorkshire, and having been popularised in ballads of the fourteenth century, has reached sites in the south and west as well. King Alfred of Wessex, who burnt the cakes – a fine example of folklore-as-history – naturally figures in his ancient kingdom. He owned land in the Vale of Pewsey, and various battle and burial traditions recall his struggle against the invading Danes. Roman generals like Vespasian and Constantius Chlorus are associated with hill-forts along with a far later general, Oliver Cromwell. The two main threads of Cromwell traditions are that he was a rampant destroyer of castles and desecrator of churches. He was certainly an efficient besieger of castles, and it is typical of folklore that he is credited with the destruction of castles which were in ruins long before the Civil War. The accusations of iconoclasm are less just, and it is perhaps through confusion with his kinsman Thomas Cromwell, who was prime mover in the Dissolution of the monasteries, that so many charges of damage done to churches have been laid at his door.

[9] T. Brown, 'The black dog' *Folklore* 69, (1958), p. 189.
[10] H. R. Ellis Davidson, 'Folklore and history', *Folklore* 85, (1974), pp. 73-92.

Various types of **assemblies** were held at some ancient sites. Camps and hill-forts were often used until the late nineteenth century as ready-made fairgrounds for trading, hiring, and indulging in rustic sports like wrestling and backswording. Occasionally the Moot site of the ancient Anglo-Saxon Hundred was a tumulus or a standing stone of some kind. Documents show that at least one such site in Wiltshire was in use as the meeting place for a court leet as late as the eighteenth century. Assemblies of a more secret kind are the sabbats held by **witches**, and on occasion an ancient site may be used as such a meeting place, though this appears to be a modern whim rather than a long-standing tradition. Leslie Grinsell stresses that only a minute fraction of Prehistoric sites are or were used for sabbats, and too much should not be made of such occurrences.[11] It is thought that witchcraft grew out of the ousting of paganism by Christianity. The old gods became the new demons and so the adherents of the old religion became convinced, as time passed, that they were worshipping the Devil, the more so since the magic they practised was frowned on the the Church. Kathleen Wiltshire notes that in some churches, fonts used to be locked to prevent witches stealing the consecrated water to use in their spells, and that such churches stand near a barrow, tumulus or sarsen stone.[12] Yet perhaps too much should not be made of this either; for in Wiltshire it is hard to find a church which is not near some kind of ancient site or stone.

Stones, as we have seen above, were once worshipped, and today some vestiges of that cult remain in folklore and even in contemporary custom. The laying of an important building's foundation stone is often accompanied by a ceremony, albeit without the mystic significance which would once have been accorded it; while since its seizure by Edward I in 1296, every British sovereign, except Mary I, has been crowned sitting upon the Stone of Scone. Perhaps the strength and endurance of stone were some of the good influences thought to be imparted by contact with it.

Stones and megalithic monuments generally have in past centuries been credited with healing powers. The feeble nature of the medical profession encouraged the populace to seek cures in charms, sympathetic magic, and the powers of sacred sites. Holed stones in particular were believed to cure diseases. The holded stone called Men-an-Tol, in Cornwall, cured rickets in the child passed through it. That stones could heal suggests a certain element of personalisation, of animism, as might be attributed to an idol. Offerings would have been made at stones, and remnants of such offerings remain in folklore. A typical example is the tradition at Wayland's

[11] L. V. Grinsell, *Folklore of Prehistoric sites in Britain*, (Newton Abbot, 1976), p. 53.
[12] K. Wiltshire, *Wiltshire Folklore*, (Salisbury, 1975), p. 2.

Smithy, a long barrow in Oxfordshire, which states that if a coin is left on the capstone and a horse tethered there overnight, Wayland Smith will have shod the horse by morning.

Another aspect of the folklore of stones which suggest their animism is the tradition, found at many stone circles, that it is impossible to count the stones and arrive at the same number twice. Anyone who by guile or magic does so, suffers a dreadful fate. The dislike of being counted is typical of supernatural beings: the magic Pigs of Cruachu could never be counted alike by different people. The inference is that by counting beings one would gain power over them. It is quite likely that this fear contributed to the public opposition to the establishment of the Census in 1801.

Animism of stones is reflected on occasion by the tendency to name two of them 'Adam and Eve', or some other names on the male/female principle. Other stones are so animate that they move, dance, or even go down to a river to drink. These activities take place nightly, daily, or at a certain time, typically when the stones hear the clock strike twelve, or hear the cock crow. Certain stones go to the other extreme and refuse to move at all. Traditions normally stress the large number of horses or oxen which were yet unable to move the stone. If moved at all by this unnaturally large team, the stone either returns to its original position of its own accord, or for some reason it is decided to return it anyway, in which case a single yoke of oxen has no difficulty moving it.

Many stone circles are said to be human beings petrified as punishment for breaking the Sabbath. The 'nine maidens', a stone circle in Cornwall, are the remains of nine girls who had the temerity to dance on a Sunday. S. P. Menefee isolates five main common factors in such legends: the number and relationship of the dancers (the seven sisters); the type of musical accompaniment (a fiddler or bagpiper); the role of the Devil; the wanton action of the dancers; and the fact that the petrifaction is less a punishment than a release from eternal dancing to the Devil's tune.[13]

Connected with many sites is the **significance of the numbers three, seven and nine.** Lambourn Seven Barrows actually comprises around forty tumuli. In many cases, these numbers are so much a part of our lives that we no longer realise their mystic significance. Yet we raise three cheers, take medicine three times daily, talk of the nine lives of a cat and a nine days' wonder, and perhaps experience the seven-year itch, or wish to sail the seven seas. The act of counting, as we have seen above, was believed

[13] S. P. Menefee, 'The "Merry Maidens" and the "Noce de Pierre"', *Folklore* 85, (1974), pp. 23-42.

to confer power on the counter, and the numbers themselves have been seen as possessing distinct innate characteristics. The significance of numbers was developed to enormous lengths in cabbalistic writings; and the occcult art of numerology, using numerical values assigned in the Hebrew fashion to the letters of the alphabet, seeks to fathom a person's character by deriving a numerical value from his name.

Treasure is said to be buried in certain conventional hiding places, in particular in the ruins of castles, hill-forts, or barrows. This was partially the result of the mediaeval practice of hiding wealth underground at times of political upheaval. A distinctive marker point was needed, and if the owner of the wealth perished subsequently, the treasure remained for some enterprising person to discover. K. Thomas notes that by the early Tudor period the excavation of barrows in the hope of quick riches was "so common that 'hill-digger' had become a recognised term of abuse for a man on the make".[14] While acknowledging that barrow-digging has gone on for centuries, and indeed was a large factor in the development of laws for treasure-trove, Leslie Grinsell particularly stresses that he knows of no instances where coins or treasure dating from the Norman or later periods were inserted into barrows.[15] Certainly, the types of treasure said to be buried in Wiltshire barrows evoke grave goods rather than coins or jewels. The practicalities of treasure-digging involve fulfilling certain conditions to ensure success; for instance, it must be dug for in silence, or even with the breath held. Sometimes it can be taken between the first or second strokes of midnight, or by throwing a sacred object at it, or when a priest recites a particular passage of scripture on a saint's day. Apart from the need to fulfill these discouraging conditions, barrow-digging involves danger from storms, from phantom horses which drive the hearer mad, or more prosaically, from breaking tools or an incensed government. Grinsell suggests that these curious traditions may be among the last survivals of pagan cults and practices.

There is a general belief among country people, noted by archaeologists of this century, that it is **ill-advised to disturb barrows**. When excavations have been interrupted by violent thunderstorms, such as that which disturbed the dig at Silbury in 1849, it serves to prove to the local people that they are justified in their awe and caution. As a result, there are a number of tales which seem designed to discourage the disturbance of barrows.

[14] K. Thomas, *Religion and the decline of magic*, (London, 1971), p. 235.
[15] L. V. Grinsell, 'Barrow treasure in fact, tradition and legislation' *Folklore* 78, (1967), pp. 1-38.

In the chapters which follow we shall be looking at individual Wiltshire sites which draw on one or several of the folklore themes considered above. While no one site will conform exactly to any given motif, it will be seen how the essential spirit of the lore remains true through all its permutations.

A   ROUND BARROWS

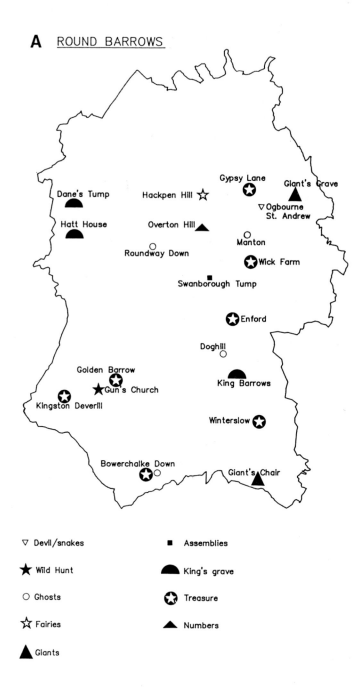

The symbols on map A give a general indication of the main types of folklore to be found at each site. Note the high proportion of burial traditions of various kinds.

FOLKLORE OF ROUND BARROWS

Round barrows do not look like graves, yet apparently local people have long recognised them as such, since the folklore associated with them relates mainly to burials, either of people or of treasure. Some idea of the preponderance of such lore connected with tumuli may be gained by comparing the map on page 20 with the maps at the end of the following three chapters. It will be seen that while treasure and burial traditions are by no means confined to one type of archaeological site, they occur most frequently in connection with tumuli.

It was said at least as early as the seventeenth century that a Danish king was buried at **Dane's Tump**, Colerne (ST/835732). Danes certainly invaded Wiltshire periodically during the Dark Ages, notably during the reigns of Alfred the Great and his brother Ethelred, and later when Ethelred the Unready was king. However, it is most unlikely that any Dane at all, much less a king, should be buried here, in what is probably a Bronze Age round barrow. It seems that, just as the antiquaries of earlier centuries attributed the ancient monuments to the earliest peoples they knew, such as the Romans or the Druids, tradition has attributed the barrow to the Danes who invaded this county long ago.

It is notable how widespread is the insistence that barrows are the graves of kings, as if some dim instinctive memory remains of the time when each tribe had its chieftain. Writing in 1901, Powell notes that among natives of south-west Wiltshire, "The dim past is called the time 'when there was a king in every county' ". The three **Hatt House barrows**, at Box (ST/834673) are said to be the graves of three kings. Mellor reports that in the 1930s, during excavations of a circular mound on nearby Totney Hill, the 'oldest inhabitant' approached him in order to tell him that "You won't find nothing here, Sir, the three kings is buried over there", pointing at Hatt House. It is usual to find that folklore is what 'the old folk believe', and the village elder was always regarded as the repository of native wit and wisdom. This is the first of several barrow groups with which the mystic numbers three and seven are associated.

More kings are buried at Amesbury. The **King Barrow** (SU/135414) doubtless was so named because of its imposing size, suited to the consequence of a king. The **Old and New King Barrows** (SU/135423) are a barrow cemetery consisting of two groups of seven, set out in straight lines. These groups were "generally called the seven kings' graves, each" when the antiquary Willian Stukeley visited them in the eighteenth century.

Another barrow cemetery lies prominent on the skyline of **Overton Hill** (SU/119683), along the line of the Prehistoric Ridgeway. Thurnam records that in a Saxon charter of the tenth century the hill appeared as 'Seofan Beorgas' (Seven Barrows), and that it was still known as 'Seven Barrowes Hill' in the seventeenth century. Osborn asserts that it is still known locally as 'Sevenbarrow Hill'. Although only seven are prominent, there are in fact around a dozen barrows here, so it seems likely that the number seven here is mystical rather than strictly descriptive.

Other burial traditions concern the type of grave goods buried rather than the actual corpse occupant. Whitlock mentions the legend that a man in golden armour was said to be buried in the **Golden Barrow** at Upton Lovell (ST/955425).[1] On occasion, excavated barrows yield finds which correspond to some extent with the folk traditions associated with them. For example, Bryn-yr-Ellyllon, the Hill of the Goblins, at Mold, Clwyd, was long said to be haunted by a soldier in a suit of gold. When the barrow was opened in 1832 it was found to cover the skeleton of a tall man wearing a corslet of bronze overlaid with gold. Similarly, the Golden Barrow, now destroyed, contained a treasure of gold plate, a cup, gold beads and buttons, and 1,000 amber beads. The name 'Golden Barrow' may have come into being after the find, but the tradition apparently predates it.

It is said that a golden table lies hidden at either **East or West Wick Farm**. Grinsell suggests that there would probably be a known pin-point for this treasure, such as the round barrow near East Wick Farm at SU/183647. The story goes that treasure seekers once found the top of the table, but when one said 'Here it is', it sank out of sight. This misfortune implies the existence of the usual condition that the treasure should have been dug for in silence.

At **Enford** is a large bowl-barrow (SU/138517) which has at some time been dug at the centre, although nothing is known of its contents. A golden chair is said to be buried beneath it: the first of three examples in this locality of this rare form of buried treasure. Grinsell was told c.1950 that visitors trying to open the barrow were stopped by local people. This may have been due simply to a healthy desire to prevent vandalism, but equally it may have been stemmed from a fear of ill consequences if the grave were to be disturbed.

When the **bowl-barrow at Gypsy Lane**, Chisledon (SU/175764) was being excavated, people came from miles around to watch, convinced that

---

[1] R. Whitlock, *In search of lost gods: a guide to British folklore,* (Oxford, 1979), p. 99.

the golden coffin said to be buried within it would be found at last. In the past, so the grandfathers said, men had dug in search of the treasure and either their tools broke, or something else happened to prevent them digging, or the 'government' stopped them. On this occasion, one very old lady begged the excavator, A. D. Passmore, not to start digging or "summat would 'appen". These are all typical consequences of barrow-digging; perhaps the most calculatedly awesome being the "summat" nameless that "would 'appen", for the nameless fear is more powerful than the concrete. Passmore was also told that the tree which grew on the barrow was "such a tree that the like has never been seen by mortal men". The tree to all appearances was no different from the others which grew nearby. Perhaps this was a more subtle attempt on the part of the local populace to prevent the dig, for in order to excavate the barrow this reputedly unique tree must be uprooted. The fear of disturbing graves is a widespread superstition. The tombs of the Pharaohs were protected by curses, and at the time of the excavation of Tutankhamun's tomb much was rumoured and written about the curse and the dire consequences of robbing a Pharaoh's grave. The descration of graves by vandals is viewed with revulsion by most people: to disturb one is at the least to show disrespect for the dead, while there is still, perhaps, a feeling that the grave is a vital part of the journey from this world to the next, and to tamper with the grave is to jeopardise the spirit's rest and transition.

In the parish of **Winterslow** (SU/230350 area), a golden coffin is reputedly buried. There are several barrows in the area and it is likely that one of these is the burial point. Another golden coffin is said to be buried beneath a **round barrow at Kingston Deverill** (ST/836369). Bronze Age burials would never have involved so incongruously modern an item as a coffin, but that one is mentioned persistently emphasises the folk awareness that these are not mere humps in the ground, but graves; and the insistence upon gold in each case suggests that such graves were known to belong to the rich and powerful.

The local conviction that barrows contained coffins is illustrated once again in a story recorded by Edith Olivier. A golden coffin was once stolen from one of the Britons' barrows. The theft was discovered, and the coffin had to be hidden; it is said to be buried somewhere on **Bowerchalke Down** (SU/020230). The story appears to be a combination of the simple buried treasure motif and that of the dangers of barrow-digging, which in this case brought eternal and supernatural punishment on the offenders, for at times seven men may be seen dragging the coffin across the downs. These seven ghostly thieves – the number is significant – are punished by an eternal search for a hiding-place for their accursed loot. A traditional punishment in legend is that of being set an impossible task. The Cornish ghost of

Jan Tregeagle, brought back from the grave to atone for his sins in life, was called upon to perform such tasks as weaving ropes from sand, clearing Berepper beach sack by sack, and emptying Dozmary Pool with a leaky shell. Spirits in the Classical underworld were tormented in a similar way: the daughters of Danaus, who slew their husbands on their wedding night, were punished by being compelled to fill a bottomless cask.

A **bowl-barrow at Manton** (SU/168689), near Marlborough, was excavated in 1906 by the Cunningtons. The barrow, some 60' in diameter, surrounded by two ditches, covered the crouching skeleton of an old woman who must have been of great importance, for with her was buried one of the richest group of grave goods in Wessex. A bronze knife with an amber pommel, beads of gold, bronze and amber, two incense cups and a collared urn with a food offering, were among the treasure found. At the time of the excavation several strange stories connected with the skeleton were in circulation.

Grinsell tells how a Mr. Bucknall of Barrow Cottage stored the ancient skeleton in his shed, and gave a friend from abroad a rather gruesome souvenir: one of the skeleton's finger-bones. Shortly after, one of his own fingers, which for some time prior to the excavation had been giving trouble, had to be amputated, and it is understood that he used his own finger to replace the one given to his friend. Subsequently the ancient skeleton, with the modern finger, was replaced in the barrow.

However, the Bronze Age lady could no longer sleep easy in her plundered grave. One of the excavators, B. H. Cunnington, relates how Dr. J. B. Maurice of Marlborough paid a professional call on a widowed lady who lived in a cottage near the barrow. The widow told the doctor that she was quite well in herself, but that "every night since that man from Devizes came and disturbed the 'old creature' she did come out of the mound and squinny into the window. I do hear her most nights and want you to give me summat to keep her away".

Dr. Maurice rose to the occasion with a nice blend of modern medicine and ancient white magic. He gave the old lady some medicine, telling her to drink a wineglass of it when it was dark, and then to go upstairs and get into bed without a light. The 'old creature', he assured her, would be fooled into thinking she had gone away, and would stop coming. Apparently he was quite right, for three weeks later the widow was able to report that after a few nights the 'old creature' had stopped disturbing her.

In the same article, Cunnington records how a London reporter visited the barrow and picked up a bone which became the focus for a séance held

Two of the Old and New King Barrows near Amesbury.

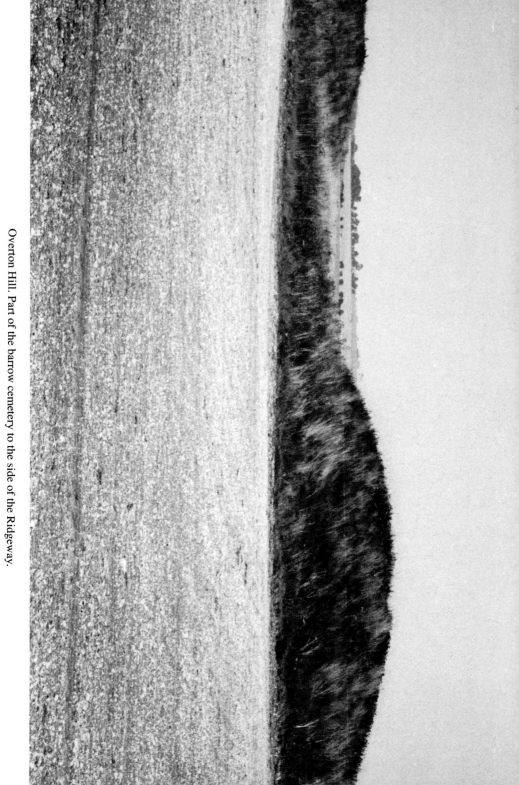

Overton Hill. Part of the barrow cemetery to the side of the Ridgeway.

The tree covered Golden Barrow near Upton Lovell.

Hackpen Hill from the west showing the white horse cut in 1838.

in Kensington. The medium obligingly saw a beautiful Saxon damsel ritually slain upon the barrow and buried within it. Doubless it made good copy, but it hardly fits the archaeological facts, since the Saxons lived some 2,000 years after the construction of the barrow. Contrasting these two last accounts, it is notable that the home-grown story is less sensational and more convincing, in its way, than that devised by the reporter. What more likely occurence, given that ghosts do walk, than that the ghost of the 'old creature' should roam abroad in search of her stolen treasure – or her finger?

The ghost which haunted a **barrow on Roundway Down** (SU/015645 area) was laid rather than disturbed by the excavation of the barrow in 1855. Prior to this date it was haunted by a man, his head under his arm, who would draw those who saw him to the almost imperceptible barrow. A local farmer named R. Coward claimed that the ghost had appeared to people he knew on three separate occasions. There are many stories of ghosts appearing to human beings in order to obtain some kind of help: often it takes the form of restoring something to its rightful owner. W. Cunnington notes that upon excavation it was found that the skeletons had been removed from several of the barrows in this area. He accounts for this by "the fact that human bones were formerly supposed to be of much value for their medical properties". Possibly the ghost was searching for its mortal remains, like the 'old creature' at Manton. Ghosts which walk without their heads are legion, and their headlessness often bears no relation to their known mode of death. Possibly the vogue for headlessness among ghosts stemmed initially from the Celtic cult of the severed head, a motif which often appears in Celtic art and sculpture, as isolated skulls found on digs, and in Celtic folklore: the head of the giant Bran the Blessed was cut off after his death and, on its own instructions, was taken back to Britain to be buried in London. "In the head rested everything that made men what they are – it was the seat of the Celtic equivalent of the soul."[2] Thus for a ghost to be headless may symbolise some essential spiritual lack which binds the soul to this earth.

Another ghost seen in the area of the barrows on Roundway Down is a black dog, whose appearance is preceded by the sound of its rattling chain, a characteristic of Wiltshire dogs. **Doghill Barrow** (SU/125455 area) due north of Stonehenge on Knighton Down, is also haunted by a ghostly dog. Katheleen Briggs notes a widespread tradition that churchyards were guarded from the Devil and witches by the Church Grim (Anglo-Saxon 'grima' signifies 'spectre'), a spirit which took the form of a black dog.[3]

[2] L. Laing, *Celtic Britain,* (London, 1981), p. 113.
[3] K. Briggs, *A dictionary of fairies,* (Harmondsworth, 1977), pp. 74-5.

The two barrow-haunting black dogs may perform the same kind of role for individual tumuli.

Spectral hounds of a more turbulent kind hunt with the ghost of the last lord of the manor of Hill Deverill. J. U. Powell records how Sir Henry Coker lived at Manor Farm beside the marsh of the river Deverill, an isolated and dreary spot. He had an ill reputation in the neighbourhood, and was said to be a smuggler and a robber. His house was little better than a den of thieves from which he and his men used to issue at night bent on robbery and worse, it seems, for it is maintained that "many went into that house that never came out", and there are said to be bloodstains on the floor of one bedroom. 'Old Coker' died in 1736, but has been absorbed onto the centuries-old tradition of the Wild Hunt, for his ghost has been seen riding through the house grounds, with "horses galloping and chains rattling". This activity is centred upon the tumulus known as **Gun's Church** (ST/891372) around which Old Coker drives his hounds to the sound of horns, chains and hoofbeats. The Wild Hunt has had many leaders since Woden. In Cornwall, the wicked priest Dando and his dogs, or alternatively, the Devil's Dandy Dogs, hunt human souls. Sir Francis Drake leads the hunt across Dartmoor. Characters like Wild Edric of Shropshire, Herne the Hunter in Windsor Great Park, King Herla of the Ancient Britons, and the Devil himself, have all been named as huntsmen. Old Coker is just one more in a long line.

In the churchyard at **Ogbourne St. Andrew**, though not actually on consecrated ground, stands a round barrow (SU/188724), reconditioned as a Norman motte-and-bailey. It is possible that the church was so sited as to Christianise the pagan burial site. Parts of the church are Norman, which does suggest that the motte-and-bailey had more influence on the church siting than the barrow itself. No earlier church is recorded in Domesday, although that does not necessarily rule out the possibility of there having been a Saxon church on this site. It was obviously of some importance, since Earl Harold held it before 1066. C. V. Goddard notes that the barrow has been avoided by local children because of the belief that it is "the abode of vipers". The snake is the traditional symbol for the Devil, and so this belief may stem from the time when priests wished to discourage attention to the pagan mound. Snakes are also associated with Avebury henge monument, where the position of the church beside the stone circle is an obvious attempt at Christianisation.

John Aubrey tells of a shepherd who lost his way one night on **Hackpen Hill** and chanced to enter a fairy hill, where he was brought into strange places underground, filled with music. Tumuli were often reckoned to be fairy hills, and this tale may well relate to the tumulus at SU/130754.

Fairyland was in some ways like the realms of the dead: a land underground, inhabited by those not of mortal kind, where time ran differently from the world above. The association of fairies with the souls of the dead, and their land underground with the underworld, would make a barrow, an ancient grave, the natural point of entry to the subterranean kingdom. As for the music, it may be coincidence, but the lower slope of Hackpen is called Fiddlers Hill, and there exist several tales, like that of the blind fiddler of Anstey, about a fiddler or drummer who enters a mysterious passage underground and is never seen again, although the sound of his playing is heard long after.

The almost imperceptible mound of **Swanborough Tump** (SU/131601) surmounted by two ash trees, was once the meeting-place of Swanborough Hundred. Ibberson notes that the ash was sacred to the Teutonic gods and that the site may be pre-Christian. Certainly it was the agreed meeting-place for Alfred and his brother King Ethelred in 878 before the battle of Ethandun, when Wessex was being attacked by Danish invaders. A passage in Alfred's will reads "when we assembed at Swanborough, we agreed, with the cognizance of the West Saxon Council, that whichever of us survived the other was to give the other's children the lands which we had ourself acquired, and the lands which King Ethelwulf gave us ..." The name 'Swanborough' took the form 'Swanabeorgh' meaning 'barrow of the peasants', in the tenth century. Significantly, three ash trees once stood atop it, but in recent years one has been blown down. As late as 1764, Swanborough Ashes or Ash was still a meeting-place for the area. "Wiltoniensis" records a document of the year which proclaims that the "tithing-man of Cheverell Parva in the said Hundred of Swanborough" was "required to be and appear before the said Steward at a Court Leet to be holden at Swanborough Ash ..." This centuries-old use of a traditional site for assemblies is paralleled in the use of hill-forts for fairs until the last century.

The size and shape of long barrows makes comparison with graves of giants quite natural, but it is unusual to find 'giant' names given to round barrows. However, at Downton we find the **Giant's Chair** (SU/163227), and at Aldbourne, the **Giant's Grave** (SU/246764). One can understand how a giant might find a tumulus a convenient place to sit, but burial in a round barrow must be uncomfortably cramped for its giant occupant. Naturally, giants are not 'dead and buried' in any normal sense, but sleep until awakened. As we shall see in the next chapter, it is possible to raise a giant living from its grave.

B LONG BARROWS AND BARROW HILLS

▲ Giant's Caves

⊛ Lugbury

◆ Hubba's Low

Silbury ▲
West Kennet ○   Marlborough
◇ ■

Adam's Grave ▼○   ▲ Giant's Grave

□
Hatfield Barrow   ▲
Giant's Grave

Giant's Grave
▲

▲ Devil		◆ Historical people
▼ Woden		■ Assemblies
○ Ghosts		□ Battles
▲ Giants		⊛ Treasure
◇ Legendary people		

Map B gives some indication of the main types of folkore to be found at each site
mentioned in chapter III. A maximum of two different types of lore is shown for each
site, when other folklore exists it is detailed in the text.

FOLKLORE OF LONG BARROWS
AND
BARROW HILLS

Neolithic long barrows are far rarer than the younger round barrows which are almost commonplace upon the Wiltshire downs. Much more impressive in size, often with huge standing stones incorporated in their structures, the long barrows invite associations with mighty giants, old gods, and demons. A glance at the map on page 28 will show how lore of supernatural, legendary and outstanding historical characters predominates.

On the hilltop above the village of Oare lies an earthwork so like a long barrow in size and shape that the local people believe it to be one. It is, in fact, the only really noticeable bank of a promontory fort, but its resemblance to a barrow has meant that it has attracted typical barrow-lore; hence it has been included in this chapter. The 'barrow' is known, predictably enough, as the **Giant's Grave** (SU/167633). As a native of Oare, I have always known that if you run seven times round the Giant's Grave, the giant will come out. I have no idea who told me this, and family and friends from Oare all say the same: 'You don't know who told you, you just know it. It's handed down.' This surely is the essence of folklore: something which is known by members of a small community, passed on so naturally and imperceptibly that the informant and transfer of information goes more or less unmarked, while the information becomes not a sensational fact, but simply an integral part of the background against which village life is set.

A genuine long barrow, some 315' long and 7' high, also called the **Giant's Grave** (SU/189582), lies on the hilltop above Milton Lilbourne, about 3¹/₂ miles south-east of the Oare Giant's Grave. The same specifications for raising the giant occur here, exact to the number of circuits of the mound taken, at a running pace. It is no surprise to find that seven circuits must be made: the number becomes monotonously predictable. The proximity of these two sites may account for the duplication of the legend, yet one feels that the same kind of thing may well be said of the long barrow, also called the **Giant's Grave**, at Downton (SU/161230), and at the many other Giant's Graves over Britain. The process for raising the buried giant is not tied to the site by further explanatory legend. It is specific, yet simple enough to be a widespread formula, which does not necessarily have to relate to archaeological sites. Village lads of Wootton Rivers near Marlborough believed that if one were to run seven times at midnight round the Big Bellied Oak in Savernake Forest, the Devil would appear.

The long barrow at Luckington, (ST/821829) was apparently discovered in 1646, according to Aubrey, who noted "there were accidentally discovered ... certain small caves, about five or six in number. They were about four foot in height and seven or eight feet long; being floored, lined and coursed with great plank-stones ..." The barrow, know as the **Giant's Caves**, has probably been so called only since its discovery in the seventeenth century. It is a gallery grave, the side chambers being the "small caves" mentioned by Aubrey. The name itself is rather puzzling, for the caves' size would be more suited to the Little People than to giants. One possible explanation is that giants were believed to have built the caves, for who but giants had the strength to use such vast building blocks? Or perhaps, over the years, the more usual 'Giant's Grave' changed into 'Giant's Cave', and later 'Caves'. The corruption of names passed on by word of mouth is common enough: the village of Stanton St. Bernard in the Pewsey Vale does not take its name from St. Bernard at all, but was originally Stanton Berners, named after the Berners family which owned land there.

The long barrow at Lanhill, near Chippenham (SU/877747) is known as **Hubba's Low**, because the Danish chief Hubba was said to have been buried there. J. Thurnam notes that in the Anglo-Saxon Chronicle for AD 878, Hubba appears to be the brother of Hynguar, and of Healfden, the ruler of the Danes of far-off Northumbria. There seems to be no evidence to suggest that Hubba was ever near Chippenham, or involved with the battle of Ethandun in 878. Thurnam traces the association to a late fourteenth-century chronicle "of little authority", written by John Brompton, Abbot of Jervaulx, in which Ethandun is dated 877, and which records: "The Danes, finding the body of Hubba among the slain, interred it with great lamentations, raising over it a mound which they call Hubbelow, which place is so called to this day, and is in Devonshire". Brompton is apparently confusing 'Hubbelow' with 'Hubbastone' or 'Whibblestone' in Devonshire. The rather confused chronicle serves merely to emphasise that a mound has been called Hubbelow for some time, and so while the explanation of the name may have originated with the imaginative abbot, the name itself did not. The element 'low', signifying a burial mound, is Danish, and so in keeping with the tale, though this is probably because, as at Dane's Tump, the mound attracted associations with the Danes as one of the most ancient peoples known to the local populace.

The chambered **long barrow at West Kennet** (SU/105677) is justly famous as one of the finest gallery graves in the country. It is 330' long and 8' high at the east end, where huge sarsen uprights form an impressive facade. The association of healing powers both with human bones and with standing stones has already been noted. In the seventeenth century, Dr. Robert Toope, of Marlborough, dug into this barrow in order to find human bones. In a letter to Aubrey, Toope claims that from these bones he made "a noble medicine that relieved many of my distressed neighbours": a telling statement which speaks volumes about the state of the seventeenth-century medical profession.

West Kennet has its own particular ghosts. At sunrise on the longest day the barrow is entered by a 'priest' followed by a huge white hound with red ears. The 'priest' is probably no more than one of those druids who were imposed on ancient sites by eighteenth-century antiquaries like Stukeley, who saw the whole Avebury complex as a vast Druidical temple given over to serpent worship. However, the white hound is worth a little attention. It is obviously not one of the family of black dogs with eyes like burning coals, but is a fairy dog, or one of their descendants. Briggs notes that apart from the Cu Sith, the green fairy dog of the Scottish Highlands, "other fairy dogs are generally white with red ears.[1]

Walker's hill near Alton Priors is crowned by a long barrow known locally as **Adam's Grave or Adam's Peak** (SU/113634). It is 200' long and 20' high, a prominent landmark for miles around, though strangely unobtrusive from some angles. As might be expected, it has acquired a fair amount of diverse folklore, of which the most obvious is its name, taken from the Christian book, and therefore, however unconsciously, Christianising a pagan site. In the nineteenth century, the barrow was known as 'Old Adam', a stone at its base being 'Little Eve'. Such male/female combinations are often a feature of ancient sites; the two remaining stones of the cove at Beckhampton are known as Adam and Eve. The barrow's earlier name, in the Saxon charter BCS 396, was 'Wodnesbeorg', meaning 'Woden's Barrow'. The Saxons who settled in the area long ago must have wondered what great figure merited so conspicuous and kingly an eternal resting place. What more likely candidate than their god Woden, who ruled the wind and storm, to whom such high places were sacred, and who must also have constructed the vast dyke nearby? There is no incongruity in the idea of a grave for an immortal god: the motif of the dying god or godlike hero is widespread throughout many mythologies. Balder the Beautiful, slain by a shaft of mistletoe, is the prime example from the Norse pantheon, while Woden/Odin was sacrificed according to his own rites, in order to win knowledge for men. "I hung from that windswept tree, hung there for nine long nights; I was pierced with a spear; I was an offering to Odin, myself to myself."[2] There are many legends of god-heroes, like our own King Arthur, who lie buried, to waken when they are called upon in

[1] K. Briggs, A dictionary of fairies, (Harmondsworth, 1980), p. 83.
[2] K. Crossley-Holland, The Norse Myths, (Harmondsworth, 1980), p. 15.

The hill at Oare which contains the bank of a promontory fort known as the Giant's grave.

Round barrow called the Giant's Chair near Downton.

The entrance to West Kennet long barrow which is entered by a huge white hound with red ears on the longest day.

Adam's Grave, or Adam's Peak, on the top of Walker's Hill near Alton Priors. A long barrow which is 200 feet long.

time of national crisis. Such great ones could never truly die, but like the giants, they sleep until wakened by those whose need and daring are great enough. Grinsell notes the familiar formula, that the giant could be raised by running seven times round the barrow, in connection with Adam's Grave. It may be inferred that the 'giant' tradition is all that remains in local memory of the once-powerful god Woden.

Two battles significant enough to appear in the Anglo-Saxon Chronicle took place at Wodnesbeorg. In 592, invaders under Ceawlin were driven off, and in 715, Ine King of Wessex and Ceolred of the Mercians fought here. The position is commanding, with the defensive frontier structure of Wansdyke to the north and the ancient Ridgeway immediately to the east. Kathleen Wiltshire records how a Miss Muriel Cobern was startled by the sound of thudding hoofbeats in the vicinity of the barrow, hoofbeats which faded as she moved away. There were no horses anywhere within sight, and it may be that, in common with the later battlefields of the Civil War, Wodnesbeorg retains some echo of the past conflicts for those to hear who can.

Lugbury long barrow (SU/831786) has been reduced from its original size by ploughing, a common fate of barrows in these days of deep-ploughing techniques. The false entrance, with its two uprights and fallen capstone, remains standing at the east end. A golden wheelbarrow is said to be buried here. It seems rather a mundane item to be be interred in a burial mound; possibly it is an agriculturalist's description of a chariot. Another explanation could be that it is an embroidered memory of the wheelbarrows used during excavations in 1825 and 1855.

Even more striking, and much rarer, than long barrows, are examples of 'barrow hills', circular mounds markedly larger than ordinary round barrows, and far more mysterious in purpose. Such mounds, of which three examples are known in Wiltshire, are not primarily burial mounds, though incidental burials may be found in them. Burl suggests that they were territorial markers, "stamping the earth with the presence of the people, each group living within its own boundaries".[3]

Within the henge monument at Marden (SU/090583) once stood the **Hatfield Barrow**, claimed to have been 20' – 50' high and over 200' in diameter. It was excavated in 1807 by the first William Cunnington, who, on sinking a conical pit from the top, failed to find any central burial. Apart from the bones of red deer, a pig and a large bird, and two human cremations, there were no signs that this was a grave, and Hoare was "inclined to think that this barrow was designed for a hill altar, or a place of general assembly, not a

[3] A. Burl, *Prehistoric Avebury*, (London, 1979), p. 13.

sepulchre". Unfortunately, the sides of the excavated pit fell in, leaving an untidy heap that a Mr. Perry levelled a few years later, so that the 'Giant of Marden' is no more. However, its folklore remains. In the fields where the barrow stood, a great treasure is said to be buried, and, according to the inevitable 'old inhabitant', it has been searched for once or twice.

A curious tradition was passed on, by a woman of an old Marden family, to the son of T. S. Cunningham, who recorded: "a great battle had been fought ages ago on Marden down between men with red heads and men with black heads, and ... the red-headed men won ... the dead were buried ina large cave on the down, and ... nobody had ever dared to enter it". There are no caves in chalk downland, of course, so 'cave' must be interpreted as a euphemism for some other burial place, such as a chambered long barrow, or indeed the Hatfield Barrow itself. Aubrey noted that the barrow had "a tradition of a fight and of some great man's being bury'd under the barrow". The strange insistence that "nobody had ever dared to enter it" would seem to put this 'cave' on a level with a fairy hill or entrance to the underworld. It is certainly a place of supernatural significance. The identity of these men with a place of supernatural significance. Timperley wonders whether the legend is a memory of Neolithic men falling to Bronze Age invaders, but more likely is the suggestion that it recalls the invasions of the Danes during the Dark Ages. Not only are folk memories of the Danes demonstrably extant in other parts of Wiltshire, as barrow names show, but apparently red-headed people in and around Marden and at Hill Deverill near Warminster have been called 'Daners' within living memory.

In the grounds of Marlborough College stands a large but rather undistinguished-looking mound (SU/184687), prosaically crowned with a water-tank. Earlier centuries have treated it with more respect. In the seventeenth century Lord Seymour cut a spiral path into it and built a summer-house and pond on the top. Earlier, in 1642, the Cromwellian defenders of Marlborough retired to the mound, then the motte of Marlborough Castle. It was the earliest part of the Norman castle, but like the barrow at Ogbourne St. Andrew which was incorporated into a motte-and-bailey structure, the mound dates from a much earlier age. The discovery of antler picks buried 2' – 3' in about halfway up the mound, makes a Prehistoric date almost certain, for these are common tools found frequently at Prehistoric sites. The **Marlborough mound** is now reckoned to be another barrow hill like Silbury.

The name 'Marlborough' derives from Anglo-Saxon 'Maerle-beorg', meaning 'Maerla's barrow', and it most probably refers to the great mound which would have dominated this part of the river-valley. Legend has confused Maerla with Merlin since the thirteenth century, for the town's motto is 'Ubi nunc sapientis ossa Merlini' or, 'Where now are the bones of the wise Merlin?' The inference is naturally that they are buried in Merlin's barrow. Merlin is one of those characters, popular in both the folklore and literature of the Middle Ages, who have left their mark in many parts of Britain in both legends and placenames. Merlin, the enchanter who prophesied for Vortigern and Aurelius Ambrosius as well as for King Arthur who succeeded them, has strong associations with Wiltshire through his legendary part in the construction of Stonehenge.

Many of the long-established agricultural and hiring fairs were traditionally held at ancient sites. Marlborough had three sheep fairs, in July, August and November, and two hiring fairs. It is possible that one or more of these fairs forms a link with ancient assemblies, held near the distinctive mound, and combining religious, social, and commercial functions. Millson records how at Jacky John's Fair, held significantly in May, people a century ago would foregather in the meadows by the river Og, then join hands and dance through the town as far as the town hall, circle round the pillars, and return to the meadows. Their dance was a variety of 'Threading the needle', in which two leaders form an arch with their arms, while other participants form two lines and run through the arch in couples, 'threading the needle' until the last couple reach the head of the line. They form a new arch, and so the players progress along the street. Christina Hole notes that this is a very old springtime game, associated especially with Shrove Tuesday and Easter.[4] Different localities have their own rhymes to accompany the game. At Marlborough the dancers chanted "The tailor's blind and he can't see, so we will thread the needle". On their return to the meadows by the Og, the procession was terminated by throwing articles into the river; an action reminiscent of some rite to placate a pre-Christian river-god. The river Og is a bourne, which often dries up in summer, so it would have been vital to ensure the god's favour for a continuous supply of water to the meadowlands nearby. Offerings made to deities of rivers, springs and wells were usually dropped into the water. In the museum of the Roman baths at Bath are displayed many small votive tokens made from semi-precious stones, which were found in the hot spring, thrown there centuries ago by the devotees of the Romano-British goddess Sulis Minerva, who presided over the springs of Aquae Sulis. The readiness with which people still throw coins into public fountains, wishing wells, and even such unlikely places as the aquarium at the zoo, demonstrates that some vestige of this custom remains with us today.

The huge Bronze Age mound of **Silbury Hill** (SU/100686) used to be the centre for a fair held on Palm Sunday, when people from the neighbouring

[4] C. Hole, *A dictionary of British folk customs*, (London, 1978), p. 71.

Marlborough mound is now covered by trees and surrounded by the buildings of Marlborough College.

The huge Bronze Age mound of Silbury Hill, once the venue for a Palm Sunday fair.

villages gathered on the hill to eat cakes and figs, and drink sugar dissolved in water from the Swallow-head spring, the source of the river Kennet. Stukeley noted the same custom in the eighteenth century, and it continued until the late nineteenth century when, like most of the great fairs held in lonely or inaccessible places, the custom gradually lapsed. A fine description of the fair as it was in its last years is given by Harvey, who compiled it from accounts given by the oldest surviving local inhabitants who attended the fair in their youth: "The roads for some little distance at the foot of the hill were occupied with stalls, on which were for sale such articles as toys, sweets, nuts, ginger beer, and more particularly flat round gingerbread cakes not gilded nor of human shape, of which it was customary to take home samples, and of Lent figs ... Hundreds of people dressed in their best clothes, from the villages round about, attended the festival. There seems to have been much merry-making and drinking. The principal amusement consisted of a rude kind of tobagganing. The young lads and lasses dragged planks of wood to the top of the hill, and then slid upon them to the bottom, much to the detriment of their nether garments".[5]

The great mound, 130' high, is reckoned to have been built in the Bronze Age, when a great stepped cone was constructed to cover a previous mound of ordinary barrow size and form. All but the last step was smoothed out with chalk, completing the imposing flat-topped mound to be seen today. Folklore, as one would expect, ascribes an entirely supernatural origin to the hill. The simplest tale, stressing a miraculous speed of construction, is that the hill was built "while a posset of milk was seething". This appears to have been a local tradition early this century, for Kathleen Wiltshire records being given this explanation in her youth by an old stonebreaker. Aubrey notes the same tale, so it would seem to be of some antiquity.

The Devil is the supernatural force responsible for the hill's construction, though its position seems to have been an accident, or at least not quite what its builder intended. The Devil is said to have dumped the hill there in a single night. Some say that it was the result of his wiping his spade while making Wansdyke. Woden was the original 'builder' of Wansdyke, so here the Devil has taken over from the old god, rather as he has taken over the leadership of the Wild Hunt in Cornwall. This Wansdyke-building account of Silbury's construction is necessarily a localised explanation, but more exist which have parallels throughout the country. There are infinite variations on this basic theme: long ago, the people of Devizes and Marlborough quarrelled. The Devil agreed to help Marlborough by dropping

[5] C. Harvey, *The ancient temple of Avebury and its gods*, (London, 1923); Review in *Wiltshire Archaeological Magazine* 42, (1922-4), pp. 380-2.

a load of earth on Devizes. Fortunately for the Devizes folk, they heard that Old Nick was coming, and appealed for help to Saint John, who just happened to be in the neighbourhood. Following his advice, a man carrying a sack of worn-out boots and shoes set off, and met the Devil near Avebury. By this time, the Devil was hot and tired, so he asked the man how far it was to Devizes. The man claimed that he had left the town years ago, and had worn out all the boots and shoes on the journey. Understandably discouraged, the Devil dumped his load and made off, thus forming Silbury Hill. Apart from explaining the origins of the hill, the tale emphasises both the vast supernatural power of the Devil, alias a religious inimical to Christianity, and the ability of wary men, aided by the wisdom of the Christian church, here represented by Saint John, to get the better of him. Further instances of the Devil's activities as hill-builder will be dealt with in the following chapter: see map C for the distribution of such sites.

Another tale, recorded by Heaney in 1913, was told to him by a member of a long-established Melksham family. "When Stonehenge was builded, a goodish bit after Avebury, the Devil were in a rare taking. 'There's getting a vast deal too much religion in these here parts,' he said, 'summat must be done.' So he picks up his shovel, and cuts a slice out of Salisbury plain, and sets off for to smother Avebury. But the priests saw him coming and set to work with their charms and incussations, and they fixed him while he were yet a nice way off, till at last he flings down his shovelful just where he stood. And that's Silbury." Quite apart from this uneducated countryman's knowledge that Avebury predates Stonehenge, this tale is remarkable because the Devil is set against whatever 'religion' was believed by the informant to be practised at Avebury and Stonehenge. The inference is that it was not Christianity, for besides the pagan sites concerned, the priests' weapons were magical "charms and incusstations", abhorrent to Christians who relied on prayer and fasting. So this is a rare instance of the Devil in combat with another religion which the Christian church would also consider devilry. Normally the Devil is found opposing Christianity, but a similar instance occurs at Treyford Hill near Midhurst in Sussex, where the adversaries are the Devil and the Norse god Thor.

Silbury Hill has been excavated several times, and there has been no burial found within it. However, legends exist of a man in golden armour, buried on horseback deep within the mound. Aubrey noted that this man was King Sil, or 'Zel' according to local pronunciation, a personage doubtless devised to account for the hill's name. Grinsell adds that Sil is buried either on horseback or in the usual golden coffin. Sil is said to be seen on some moonlit nights riding his horse around the hill; while a headless ghost is also seen there.

The local people seem to have looked with characteristic disfavour on excavations of Sil's burial place. Dean Merewether of Hereford tells of a violent thunderstorm which greeted the end of the excavations of 1849. The storm was "much to the satisfaction ... of the rustics, whose notions respecting the examination of Silbury and the opening of the barrows were not divested of superstitious dread". Thunder and lighting have long been believed to have a supernatural origin. Zeus and Jupiter used thunderbolts as weapons, while Thor was called 'the Thunderer', and created thunder and lighting with the blows of his mighty hammer Mjöllnir. Thus there could be little more apt than a thunderstorm to signify supernatural displeasure at the disturbance of graves.

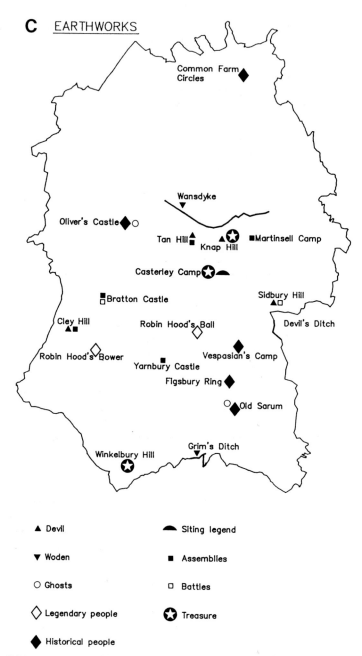

C EARTHWORKS

Common Farm Circles ◆

Wansdyke ▼

Oliver's Castle ◆○

Tan Hill ▲▪ ▲★ ■Martinsell Camp
Knap Hill

Casterley Camp ★ ◜

■Bratton Castle
□

Sidbury Hill
▲□

Cley Hill
▲■

Robin Hood's Ball ◇   Devil's Ditch

Robin Hood's ◇ Bower

Vespasian's Camp ◆
■
Yarnbury Castle

Figsbury Ring ◆

○◆ Old Sarum

Grim's Ditch
▼
Winkelbury Hill ★

▲ Devil   ◜ Siting legend

▼ Woden   ■ Assemblies

○ Ghosts   □ Battles

◇ Legendary people   ★ Treasure

◆ Historical people

Map C illustrates generally the main types of folklore attached to each site. Folklore of earthworks is particularly diverse but perhaps the most notable aspects are camps as the sites of past assemblies, and the legendary involvement of the Devil in creating dykes and hill forts.

FOLKLORE OF EARTHWORKS

Wiltshire's ancient earthworks range from Neolithic causewayed camps and the simpler Iron Age hill-forts to frontier dykes, some of which still lie on our modern county boundaries. Their folklore on the one hand comprises mysterious tales of buried treasure, demonic activity, associations with various historic and semi-mythical personages, and siting legends; while on the other hand it recalls the fairs and gatherings held in the hilltop enclosures upon religious and agricultural festivals. The map on page 38 will give an overall picture of the diversity of earthwork-lore.

The enclosure on **Knap Hill** (SU/122636) is an excellent example of a Neolithic causewayed camp, its bank and ditch being interrupted by five causeways. It lies upon the opposite side of the Ridgeway to Adam's Grave, or Saxon Wodnesbeorg. On the north side of the camp is a small triangular Romano-British earthwork, which upon excavation showed signs of having been burnt out. A sixth-century Saxon sword was one of the finds. The enclosure may well have been burnt out during the slaughter at Wodnesbeorg in AD591. A slight bank, looking like a wide cart track, emerges from the rampart of Knap Hill, and descends the steepest part of the hill, ending at its foot; the last yards are almost sheer. The best place to view this bank is from the road which leads from the Altons up the hill, passing between Adam's Grave and Knap Hill. From this distance the bank is clearly visible but at close quarters it is almost impossible for the untrained eye to see; to all intents and purposes, it vanishes. Such suspicious and uncanny behaviour has earned it the title of the **Devil's Trackway**, the Devil being the base master of disguise, trickery and shape-shifting.

During the excavations of 1908-9, M. E. Cunnington learned of the local belief that treasure was buried here. Legends of treasure are by no means confined to barrows. Other hill-forts in Wiltshire have such legends, and in their case it cannot be easily explained away as a memory of grave goods. However, there are always barrows near hill-forts, and it is possible that over the years the folklore has become detached from one type of site and settled on the other.

The case of **Winklebury Hill** (ST/952215) might serve to illustrate this transfer of lore in progress. The hill is topped by a promontory fort, and there are round barrows close by. The landlord of the nearby Talbot Inn told Leslie Grinsell c. 1950 that a golden coffin was buried somewhere on the hill. One suspects that the coffin used to rest in one of the barrows; recently, like St. Cuthbert's coffin, it has been on the move, and possibly by now it will have reached the hill-fort.

The golden chair reputed to be buried in **Casterley Camp** (SU/115535) is rather more puzzling. It is notable that the nearest 'treasure barrow' in the vicinity is the round barrow at Enford, also said to contain a golden chair. The two may be connected in some way: perhaps the barrow legend gave rise to the hill-fort tradition, or possible they both recall some tale, now forgotten, of a golden chair.

A remarkable tradition connecting Casterley Camp with the village of Upavon was noted by the Cunningtons: it was said that the village once stood upon the hilltop, and that the people moved down and built Upavon. This tale was traditional at the time of the Cunningtons' excavation, and given that "before the site was excavated no-one would have thought of describing it as that of a deserted village"[1], one is left wondering just how long country memories are. The camp is reckoned to date from the early first century AD, a time when Roman invaders under the future Emperor Vespasian were moving through the south of Britain, demolishing hill-forts and moving the tribes into new settlements. One cannot discount the possibility that the tradition may recall just such an enforced move.

That industrious evil-doer, the Devil, is responsible for creating **Sidbury Hill** (SU/216505), for he dropped it when he got tired of carrying it on his way from Bristol to London. Quite why he had burdened himself with a hill-sized chunk of earth is not specified, but by analogy with more detailed tales of this type, one assumes that the Londoners had offended his infernal sensibilities – too many churches, perhaps – and he planned to crush their pretensions in his usual way by dropping a hill on them. Fortunately for London, he gave up the attempt without even having to be tricked.

There is an Iron Age hill-fort on Sidbury Hill, and locals believed that there was once a battle here, for the nearby barrow cemetery on **Snail Down** (SU/218522) is said to be the resting place of "the people killed in the battle of Sidbury Hill". The defensible hill-fort would be the centre for any battle here.

Besides learning of this battle tradition during his excavations at Snail Down in 1953, Thomas met with local disapproval at his barrow-digging activities. A 77-year-old shepherd informed him that when the first William Cunnington had done similar excavations in 1805, he had been put in prison as a result. The old shepherd had heard the story from a man who had actually been present at Cunnington's dig and this tale demonstrates how quickly, and with how few informants, fact can be transformed into

[1] M. E. Cunnington, *An introduction to the archaeology of Wiltshire*, (Devizes, 1933), p. 38.

The Neolithic causewayed camp on Knap Hill seen from Walker's Hill.

Winklebury Hill which is topped by a promontory fort.

Cley Hill with the ramparts of its Iron Age hill fort.

The Westbury White Horse with the earthworks of Bratton Castle on the skyline above.

folklore. The tale is preposterous, and a typical example of a cautionary tale produced in an attempt to stop interference with the barrows.

Only a few miles east of the two golden chairs of Casterley Camp and the Enford round barrow, we find yet another example of this rare form of buried treasure. A well in Everleigh is said to have an opening in its side, and from it a tunnel leads to Sidbury Hill. In the tunnel stands a golden chair. Most legends of tunnels prove to be fabrications, and in any case the presence of a golden chair – unlikely furniture for any tunnel – must denote its mythical state. However, south of Everleigh, a fairly well-preserved linear earthwork runs from a series of banks and ditches beneath the Weather Hill Firs (SU/219521) to Sidbury hill-fort. This bank and ditch could be the origin of the 'tunnel'. Hoare notes the linear earthwork and writes of his hopes of discovering "the traces of King Ina's palace, who according to tradition, had a country seat at Everley". The tradition is interesting in view of the existence of the banks and ditches beneath the firs, earthworks which have yielded no evidence of actual settlement, but which may indeed have had some connection with Ine King of Wessex from 688 to 726. Perhaps the tradition of the golden chairs sets the stamp of the throne of Wessex upon this area.

West of Warminster lies **Cley Hill** (ST/838449), an imposing isolated hill with a spur, known as little Cley Hill, pointing north-east. The main bulk of the hill is crowned by a very prominent Iron Age hill-fort, on which stand tumuli visible from the low ground. The full effect is that of a hat or beret set on a bald head, and this probably gave rise to the saying:

"Big Cley Hill do wear a hat.
Little Cley Hill do laugh at that."

Cley Hill is another geographical feature which is attributed to the Devils ill-will. The following account, in broad Wiltshire dialect, is another variation of the theme discussed on pages 35 – 36, with reference to Silbury Hill, where the Devil is foiled by quick thinking on the part of a mortal man. 'The Vize' and 'The Vizes' are local names for Devizes, and these forms recall the original name 'Apud divisas', meaning 'at the boundaries', the town being created at the point where the boundaries of the manors of Potterne and Cannings meet. Once again the Devizes folk are the target of Satan's fury: "The Vize vawk had offended the Devil mainly, an' a swore he'd sar'em out. So a went down the country, an' vound a girt hump an' a putt it on's back, an' a carr'd it along to vling at 'em. An' a came along be Warminster, an' a met a man an' a zays to 'im, "Can 'ee tell I the rhoad to Vizes?" an' tother zaid, "Lor thur now, that's just what I do want to knaw myself, for I started to look for un when my beard wur black an' now a's grey, an' I hant a got there 'it." "Lor! says the Devil ('twer the Devil 'snaw) if that's how tes I beant a gwine to car thick no vurder," an' a flung thick girt hump off's shoulder an' thur a bee, look'ee see. An' that's how Cley Hill got thur."[2]

A revel used to be held on Cley Hill on Palm Sunday, and here we find another link with the Devil, for there was a custom of burning the grass "to burn the Devil out". Another aspect of this revel was a form of the game known as 'bandy', a kind of hillside hockey, in which a line of people armed with curved sticks would be ranged up the hill, and attempt to hit a ball from the bottom to the top. Wiltshire seems to have had a tradition of fairs on Palm Sunday, all held on chalk hilltops, as at Silbury or here at Cley Hill, and often involving energetic hillside sports like bandy and summer tobogganing. None of these fairs seems to have survived long into the twentieth century, for not only were the sites somewhat inaccessible, but the riotous nature of the merry-making offended late-Victorian morality.

One of the two round barrows within the camp on Cley Hill is endowed with a very curious piece of folklore. It is said to be inhabited by the guardian spirit of the folk of the neighbouring parish of Bugley. This benevolent spirit would direct people to a local well, whose water cured weak eyes. Probably this guardian spirit, now dwindled to little more than a helpful solitary fairy, was once a local minor deity, who presided over a local tribe and their sacred well whose water had magical properties. Place-name etymology may tie in with this legend, for while Bugley probably derives from 'Bucges leah' meaning 'Bucge's clearing or wood', the expert acknowledges "the possibility that this name contains Middle English 'bugge', 'hobgoblin' ".[3]

Like many hill-forts, Cley Hill has links with one of the popular historical leaders of the distant past. King Alfred and his army are said to have "gone up there". Prior to the battle of Ethandun in 878, Alfred's forces certainly encamped at Iley Oak near Warminster, and in all probability they would have made some use of Cley Hill's commanding prospect over the surrounding countryside.

A few miles from Cley Hill lies the village of Edington, and to the south of the village rise the slopes of Edington hill, now thought to be the 'Ethan-dun' or 'waste down' of the battle where Alfred won his decisive victory over Guthrum's Danes. However, tradition maintains that nearby **Bratton Castle** (ST/510905) was the battlefield, and that the famous

[2] C. V. Goddard, 'Wiltshire folklore jottings', *Wiltshire Archaeological Magazine* 50, (1942 – 4), p. 31.
[3] J. E. Gover et al, *The place-names of Wiltshire*, (Cambridge, 1939), p. 158.

Westbury white horse beneath the earth ramparts was cut as a memorial of the victory. Morris Marples asserts that this tradition probably dates only from the eighteenth century, having originated with Plenderleath, the antiquary so interested in hill-figures.[4] Certainly the present white horse dates only from the eighteenth century, when Lord Abingdon's steward, suitably named Mr. Gee, remodelled (Fig. 2) the bizarre piece of equine art which preceded it. (Fig. 3) Was this dachsund-like beast really cut by Alfred's victorious solders? It would be agreeable to think also, and that, like the ancient Uffington horse, its stylised form bears the hallmarks of the genuine article. The crescent moon at the tip of the tail does recall the crescent moons found above the backs of stylised horses which appear on coins of the period. However, there is apparently no evidence to show that this earlier horse is more than an eighteenth-century folly. Marples notes that "Writers like Camden, Aubrey and Baskerville, who mention the Uffington horse, are completely silent as to what must have been the equally

Westbury white horse, as it is today.
After M. Marples

Westbury white horse, before recutting
After Gough, in M. Marples

remarkable Westbury figure." When one considers how widespread was the eighteenth-century love of building fake 'antiquities', the likelihood of a landowner having seen the Uffington horse and having a similar figure cut on his land cannot be dismissed out of hand. Probably the true tale will never

[4] M. Marples, *White horses and other hill figures*, (Gloucester, 1981), p. 68.

be known, but genuine or fake, it is sad that the spirited stallion should have been usurped by Mr. Gee's soulless nag.

Chalk figures have to be regularly scoured or they become overgrown and eventually disappear altogether. A revel used to be held at the time of the scouring at Bratton. If the earlier horse was truly ancient, this revel might have been a survival of an earlier celebration, but if, as seems more likely, the horse is an eighteenth-century imitation, the revel was probably instituted as an imitation in its turn of the Uffington 'pastime'. It is worth noting in passing that the Uffington gathering was held every seven years.

A more modern general, but one who has been widely absorbed into folklore owing to the geographical range of his activities, is Oliver Cromwell. **Oliver's Castle**, or **Camp** (SU/001647), an Iron Age hill-fort near Devizes, is named after this much-maligned commander. In the autumn of 1643, following the arrival of reinforcements, the Royalist defenders of Devizes under Prince Maurice broke the three-day siege, and engaged the Parliamentary troops under Sir William Waller on Roundway Down. The Roundheads, already exhausted by the previous battles, were thoroughly routed by the Cavaliers, and driven over the edge of the steep escarpment. Many of them met their deaths when their horses fell, driven beyond endurance down the breakneck slope. Some claim that on still nights the screams of these long-dead men and horses can still be heard. This is hardly as dramatic as the phantom battle of Edgehill, where the whole encounter was frequently re-enacted in the sky above the field, but it is obviously a haunting in that tradition.

Oliver's Castle is yet another hill-fort said to contain treasure. Leslie Grinsell was told by local lads that explorers had been examining the ground with mine detectors searching for the golden coffin. It is quite possible that people with metal detectors might feel that the ancient camp would be an ideal spot for a little treasure-hunting, and the local lads doubtless concluded that since people were searching, it must be for the valuable coffin which, as everyone knew, was buried there. In the same way excavators like Passmore at Chisledon have been regarded as digging for treasure, rather that from archaeological motives.

Before leaving Oliver's Castle, it must be observed that Oliver Cromwell probably never came near the fort named after him. He was almost certainly never at Highworth either, but an old man once asserted that Cromwell and his army used one of the **Common Farm group of earthen circles** (SU/210932) to camp in when attacking Highworth.

Roundway Down and the Iron Age hill fort of Oliver's Castle.

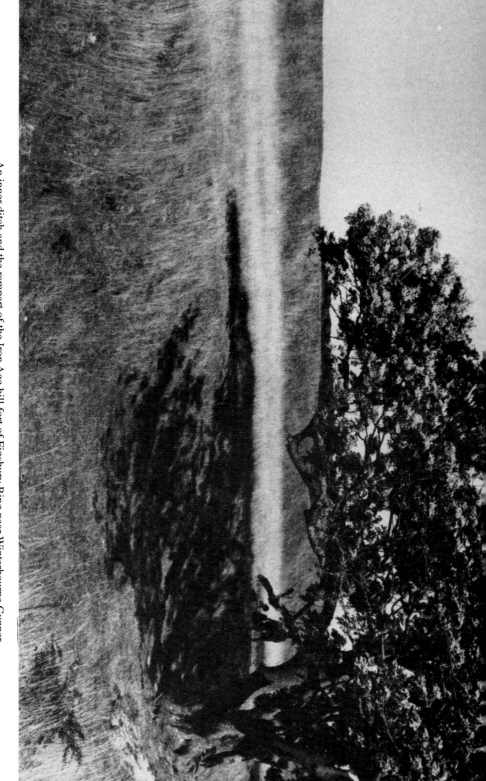

An inner ditch and the rampart of the Iron Age hill fort of Figsbury Ring near Winterbourne Gunner.

An old trackway from Steeple Langford leads to the Iron Age hill fort of Yarnbury Castle, once the site of an annual sheep fair.

Part of the inner bailey and gateway of Old Sarum.

Like many such characters, Cromwell has acquired the credit for doing things which historical records prove ill-founded. For example, local belief maintains that Cromwell fired at Highworth church from Castle Hill, Blunsdon, a distance of three miles away, and actually hit the church. The tale seems devised to illustrate Cromwell in his popularly-ascribed role of iconoclast, for as Allan and Passmore point out, quite apart from the fact that Cromwell was probably not there anyway, the seventeenth-century field guns had a range of less than half that distance. In this way, folk heroes and villains gain a reputation for deeds which are larger-than-life, while some eventually become giants in stature to match their reputation. In 1190, when the Glastonbury monks found what they took to be King Arthur's coffin, the bones inside were said to be larger than those of an ordinary man. The shin-bone was longer by three fingers than the shin of the tallest monk. Arthur's stature had grown in proportion to his reputation.

The Iron Age hill-fort called **Figsbury Ring** (SU/188338) was excavated by M. E. Cunnington, who noted that its alternative name was **Chlorus' Camp**. This name seems to have been popularised by Stukeley, who accepted Bishop Kennet's theory that the Romano-British general Constantius Chlorus, father of the Emperor Constantine, had enlarged the existing camp, which henceforth was named 'Chloren' after him. Even if this name dates only from the eighteenth century it has become local usage, and it illustrates the tendency of early antiquarians to associate the earliest likely civilisation they knew with ancient sites. In spite of Stukeley's obsession with 'restoring' monuments to the druids, he must have felt that the martial Romans were a more likely choice in the case of hill-forts. Likewise, he attributed **Vespasian's Camp** (SU/145417) near Amesbury, and **Yarnbury Castle** (SU/035404), both Iron Age hill-forts, to the general who was later to become the Emperor Vespasian of Rome. The more realistic Hoare rightly ascribes these camps to the 'Britons', but concedes "that this great General occupied one or both of them, during his conflicts with the Belgae, is not unlikely".[5]

Robin Hood, a legendary character who is now reckoned to have his origins in a human being rather that the woodland spirit Robin Goodfellow, is yet another figure after whom sites throughout the country are named. His home territory is the Midlands around Sherwood Forest in Nottinghamshire. This does not prevent two Wiltshire earthworks, the Neolithic causewayed structure called **Robin Hood's Ball** (SU/109463), and a circular structure called **Robin Hood's Bower** (ST/877423), from bearing his name. He is one of those figures who appeal to the popular mind for reasons heroic or

[5] R. C. Hoare, *Ancient history of south Wiltshire*, (London, 1812), p. 160.

villainous, and who, like the gods of old, are paid tribute in the names of prominent local sites.

The deserted city of **Old Sarum** (SU/138327) has had a chequered history. Since the original Iron age hill-fort was built on this commanding site it has been occupied by people of the Iron Age, Romans, Saxons, Danes and Normans. A woman visitor to Old Sarum in 1967 claims to have seen a boy amusing himself by swinging from one of the old yew trees which then grew on the outer earthworks. This was not unusual in itself, but the boy, his hair short and tousled, was dressed in a rought brown tunic and short brown cloak, with lighter leggings of hose cross-gartered to the knee, and sandals on his feet. The apparition must have been extremely vivid for the witness to have gained so detailed an impression of his appearance, as it seems the boy vanished almost immediately.

In the twelfth century, friction developed between the city and the ecclesiastical community, whose cathedral lay outside the city walls. The clerics were dependent on the goodwill of the city governors for their movements in and out of the walled fortress. There were other aggravations, among them the high winds which damaged the cathedral and drowned the voices of those celebrating divine office, the shortage of water available once again only by the goodwill of the city governor, and at a price he set, and the whiteness of the chalk ramparts which, it was somewhat hysterically claimed, caused blindness among the clergy. The final straw occurred in 1217 when the Dean and clergy returned from a Rogationside service in St. Martin's church, Milford, only to find the east gate of the city barred against them. They were forced to remain outside for the night. Fortunately Bishop Poore obtained papal and royal permission to move to a spot where the community could be independent, down in the fertile valley of the Avon. The choice of site, according to legend, was decided when an archer, standing on the city ramparts, drew his bow and shot an arrow a miraculous distance of two miles into the watermeadows below. The event was seen as divine guidance, and it was decided to build the new cathedral on the spot where the arrow fell. This tradition may explain why so vast an edifice as the cathedral should have been built in a watermeadow which was frequently flooded by the Avon. However, one suspects that the fact that the Bishop owned that particular watermeadow may have had some influence on the arrow's flight.

Another of the Palm Sunday fairs used to be held in **Martinsell Camp** (SU/177639), an Iron Age hill-fort at the south-east corner of Martinsell Hill between Oare and Wootton Rivers. Like the fairs at Silbury and Cley Hill, sports and games were the order of the day. Some recruiting seems to have taken place, and a local lad who joined up went off to serve in the

Crimean War and the Siege of Sebastpol. As at Cley Hill, bandy was played up the escarpment, and boys scrambled for oranges down it. The most bizarre sport was the practice of sliding down the almost perpendicular hillside seated on the skulls or jawbones of horses. It will be recalled that the young folk would slide down Silbury Hill, but the addition of the grotesque toboggans adds a dimension seen by some as the vestiges of an ancient pagan horse cult, of which the hobby horses and their Welsh equivalent, the Mari Lwyd, or grey mare, with its horse skull head, are also part. Be that as it may, in the nineteenth century the church obviously took no account of any pagan element, for the tale is told of "a certain grave episcopal and academic dignitary" who was persuaded to launch himself down the slope without even a jawbone, was unable to stop, and landed safe but rather battered in the Pewsey Vale below. Besides the strenuous sports, quarrels were settled by fighting and wrestling, a practice which led to the fair's decline, for it was frowned on as being too violent and rowdy. For some years after the fair's closure around 1860, a church service with a brass band was held in its place.

The fort continued to be a favourite spot for games and was known as "the children's playground" from the custom of spending every fine Saturday there.

Yarnbury Castle (SU/035404), already mentioned for its supposed connection with Vespasian, was until around the end of the nineteenth century the site of an annual sheep fair. Within the Iron Age fort, with its elaborate in-turned east entrance, can be seen the marks which show where the sheep pens used to stand. The fair held here must have been very similar to that which took place on **Tan Hill** (SU/082647) each 6th August. There is no fort or barrow on Tan Hill, but it is the highest hill in Wiltshire, reaching 964', and is surrounded by tumuli, hill-forts and Wansdyke. Its position in local folklore, and the air of mystery popularly surrounding it, mark it out as an ancient site indeed. The gathering held on Tan Hill was both a sheep and horse fair, and a general holiday. At one time even roundabouts were set up here. Broad beans were boiled on the spot in water from the nearest dewpond, and sold at 'a penny a perch' – as many as could be stabbed by a three-pronged fork. By tea-time the commerical dealings were over and then the merry-making got well under way. At last the fair got so rowdy that "decent girls were gated on that day", and finally like other hilltop fairs, it died a natural death.

Controversy reigns over the derivation of the hill's name. The more prosaic view is that 'Tan' is a corruption of 'St. Anne', who is the patron saint of the nearby parish church of All Cannings, while the date of the fair, 6th August, is St. Anne's day, old style. On some maps the hill is marked 'St. Anne's Hill', and according to one local writer, Ralph Whitlock, this is the earliest documented form of the name. The more colourful theory, expounded by Story-Maskelyne [6], is that Tan Hill is the original form, named after Tan or Tein, a Celtic fire-god. 'Tan', the Celtic for 'fire', becomes Santan, the holy fire, later Christianised to Saint Anne, who is the special patroness of Celtic Brittany. St. Anne's day is, according to Story-Maskelyne, significantly near 1st August, the Celtic festival of the first-fruits, known as Lugnasad. Hence she concludes that Tan Hill fair's origins lie in a Celtic fire festival. It is a chicken-and-egg situation: was the saint's name derived from the god's or vice versa? Since precedence will probably never be satisfactorily established, people are free to conjecture as they wish and to continue to endow the hilltop with mysterious legends. Kathleen Wiltshire notes the rumours of witchcraft rites involving the cremation of a black cock, and continues "certainly the ash from the fire was saved: it was, among other things, considered a cure for scour in calves (dysentery), and good fertiliser for plants". Perhaps these tales of black and white magic have some foundation on fact, for on an old map in Devizes museum the highest peak is marked the Devil's Church, suggestive of a centre of witchcraft, or perhaps an early pagan holy place. Kathleen Wiltshire also notes that a white chalk scar in the hillside is said to be be the mark of the Devil's Spade.

Another strange tale concerns a girl of about twelve years of age, who, in the early 1960s, took her dog for a walk near Wansdyke on Tan Hill. On her return home she asked who lived in a house she had seen there, and she described the stable adjoining it, with a horse looking out over the half door at the hens scratching for food. Not even the oldest shepherds had ever heard of a house on Tan Hill, and when the girl returned to look for it, there was nothing there. A few years later a relative borrowed a library book on Wiltshire, which contained old illustrations. One showed a view of a house standing beside a track on Tan Hill.

Wansdyke is a vast frontier bank and ditch which runs across the Marlborough Downs from Morgan's Hill (SU/023672) to Savernake forest (SU/196665), following more or less the line of the south escarpment of the downs, and passing sites like Tan Hill, Rybury Camp, Adam's Grave and Knap Hill. Its earlier name was 'Wodnes dic', Woden's Dyke, for the Saxons must have thought that only one as mighty as a god could have constructed it. Nowadays it is reckoned to be post-Roman, since it cuts across the line of a Roman road. In the eighteenth century, as a print by Stukeley shows, there was a gibbet on Wansdyke where it crosses Morgan's Hill. It is an interesting concidence, if concidence it is, for Woden was the god of the dead and sacrifices made to him were by hanging.

[6] T. Story-Maskelyne, 'Tan Hill Fair', *Wiltshire Archaeological Magazine* 34, (1905–6), pp. 426-32.

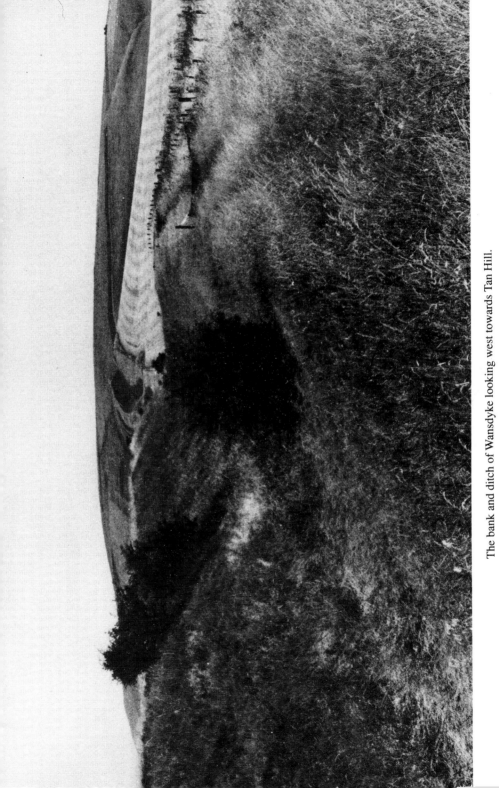

The bank and ditch of Wansdyke looking west towards Tan Hill.

The line of Grim's Ditch on the Wiltshire/Dorset border is marked by trees and bushes near Swayne's Firs.

At the beginning of the century three shepherds guarding their flock on Tan Hill saw perhaps the most intriguing phantoms in Wiltshire. One moonlit night they heard the sound of men and horses approaching along Wansdyke; and that was strange enough on the lonely downs. But the party which was approaching was remarkable at any time and place: a party of men carrying flaming torches, escorted a wagon drawn by black horses. A coffin lay on the wagon, and upon the coffin was a golden crown. As this group drew level with the shepherds it vanished. The same cortège was seen by a man on Wansdyke near Huish. Kathleen Wiltshire, who relates these tales, subscribes to the view that the cortège is that of Queen Guinevere being taken on the safe route over the downs to her grave in Glastonbury: it is, at least, a charming interpretation.

Wansdyke is unique to the county of Wiltshire, but in many other counties can be found stretches of linear earthworks, and many bear the name Grim's Ditch, or Devil's Ditch. Around Salisbury are various stretches of such dykes. **Grim's Ditch**, in keeping with its function as a frontier structure, follows the county boundary between Wiltshire and Dorset from SU/051220 to SU/127235, as does a shorter section from SU/131207 to SU/136214. The local alternative name for these earthworks is the Devil's Ditch, and inversely, the Devil's Ditch north of Cholderton (SU/215450 area to SU/228462 area) is also known as Grim's Ditch. 'Grim' derives from Anglo-Saxon 'grima', meaning 'spectre' and its adjective 'grim', meaning 'fell' or 'dire'. Hence by implication it recalls that giant or demon which was reckoned to have built the work. However, Grim and Grimnir were by-names of Odin/Woden, the god destined to become a devil under the Christian faith. In this area where the concentration of Woden names suggests the existence of some centre of his cult, 'Grim' may well refer specifically to the god rather than to some anonymous supernatural being.

Avebury▲○ Fyfield Down ●

▲○
Devil's Den

● Hanging stone

Kinwardstone ▲△

Bulford
▲△

Stonehenge▲◇ Cholderton ▲

■ Kingston Deverill

▲△ East Knoyle

▲ Devil	● Sheep
○ Ghosts	△ Immovable stones
◇ Legendary people	■ Assemblies

When compared to maps A, B and C, map D demonstrates the individuality and specialised nature of stone-lore. Devil-names and traditions predominate, along with various properties of stones, of which immovability is the chief.

FOLKLORE OF STANDING STONES AND HENGES

In pre-Christian times, stones of significant size were worshipped, and that this stone cult continued well into the ninth century AD is evident from the edicts of various councils, such as the late ninth-centry Edict of Nantes, all of which condemn the workship of stones, and declare that those who neglect to destroy them are guilty of sacrilege. From this stone cult and the Church's condemnation of it come the main strands of stone-lore: the power and animate will of stones, and their associations with the Devil. Stones worshipped as idols would become in some sense animate, and possessed of certain of the attributes of the living, such as the power to bless, curse, move, hear and heal. Later, the Church would call the veneration of stones the worship of the Devil, and so were born tales of the Devil trying to move stones, build with them, or use them as weapons against the Church. The map on page 50 gives some indication of how the Devil is most closely associated with these most tangible symbols of his former sovereignty.

Sandstone rocks known as **Sarsen stones**, like those on Fyfield Down (SU/140704), occur naturally and in great numbers in Wiltshire. Their name reflects their pagan associations, for 'sarsen' is reckoned to be a corruption of 'saracen', the name given to heathens or pagans in the Middle Ages. So these are heathen stones, and used in the construction of heathen monuments. It is significant that the Rollright Stones in Oxfordshire are also sometimes called sarsen stones, though they are of oolitic limestone. Locally the sarsen stones are called 'grey wethers', because "in a dusky evening, they look like a flock of sheep".[1] Even this simple simile accepts a certain element of life in the stones. As to their origins, while Sir Christopher Wren thought that they were cast up by a volcano, Samuel Pepys describes them as "stones of considerable bignes (sic), most of them certainly growing out of the ground". Pepys was expressing the popular belief which still existed in the 1940s, as Goddard notes: "The older generation firmly believed, and do still, that the loose stones in the soil grow there, rather like potatoes".

Such a belief is understandable in chalk downland where any ploughed field in mottled with flints, as if the farmer had purposely set out to cultivate them. A stone at Stone Farm, Blaxhall, Suffolk, is said to have been the size of a small loaf a century ago, and subsequently to have grown to its present weight of five tons. Such tales serve to emphasise a basic belief that stones, which are the very bones of Mother Earth, have life of their own.

[1] J. Aubrey, *Monumenta Britannica*, (Sherborne, 1980), p. 18.

In south Wiltshire are, or were, several isolated stones associated with the building of Stonehenge by the Devil. At **Cholderton**, in the Devil's Ditch, lay a stone dropped by the Devil as he was flying over to Stonehenge. Although the Cholderton stone seems no longer to be there, it was probably the one at Park Gate (SU/232435), seen by Jackson in the 1880s. He noted the tradition that the Stonehenge sarsens came from Andover across the county boundary in Hampshire, and that this stone had been abandoned on the way.

Another stone dropped by the Devil on his way to Stonehenge used to lie in the river Avon at **Bulford** (SU/165440), but has been removed to the garden of a house near Bulford bridge. It is of oolitic limestone and can have no connection with the great sarsens and bluestones of Stonehenge. However, it has gathered other typical stone-lore: it is (or was) an immovable stone. An 'observer' wrote to the *Salisbury Times* in 1910 that "several attempts have been made to drag the stone away from the river. Forty, and some say sixty oxen were employed, but it was never even moved". Such incredible assertions are designed to stress the vast supernatural power and will which such stones were believed to possess. Another attribute of this stone which again stresses its determination to remain in its chosen position, but which cheerfully contradicts the previous piece of stone-lore, is that if the stone were turned over, it always righted itself. The awe with which the stone was regarded locally is similar to the reverence shown to barrows. When the stone was removed from the river, "those employed in the work were at first reluctant to have anything to do with it".

In a field near **East Knoyle** (ST/882312) is a large irregular stone, of which "they do say as Old Nick dropped it there, when he was carrying it to build Stonehenge".[2] It was also said that many horses had been employed in an attempt to move it, without success; not surprisingly since there is supposed to be as much stone below ground as above. A similar stone is the monolith at Rudston, Yorkshire, said to measure around 50' in height, 25' above and below ground. Such tales may again be designed to stress the stone's deep-rooted determination to remain where it is despite the efforts of hostile people to destroy or uproot it. The Rudston monolith seems to have won its struggle: it stands unmoved in the churchyard to the north of the church, on the side where the north or 'Devil's' door would be.

West of Marlborough, in Clatford Botton, stands the **Devil's Den** (SU/152697), a cromlech consisting of four sarsen uprights with a capstone. These are the remains of a simple chamber set at the end of a Neolithic long

[2] G. H. Skipworth, 'Folklore jottings from the western counties', *Folkore* 5, (1894), pp. 339-40.

Sandstone rocks, known as sarsen stones, on Fyfield Down.

Stone at East Knoyle said to have been dropped by Old Nick when building Stonehenge.

The Devil's Den in Clatford Bottom to the west of Marlborough.

The Hanging Stone in the field known as Hanging Stone Hurst in Alton Barnes parish.

barrow, now destroyed. Whenever horses or oxen were harnessed to pull away the capstone, the chains would break. This is hardly surprising, for the great capstone is reputed to weigh seventeen tons. At midnight the Devil yokes four white oxen to it and tries to move it; so far, in vain. He is watched by a great white dog with eyes like burning coals, which peers from beneath the capstone. Possibly this dog is related to the fairy dog, white with red ears, which inhabits the West Kennet long barrow nearby.It could also have had red ears originally, but over the years, and by analogy with the more usual black dog with eyes like burning coals, the red ears may have become red eyes. However, there seems some doubt whether the beast which watches the Devil is a hound at all. A. G. Bradley's version of the tale is that Satan's companion is a white rabbit, also "with lurid coals for eyes", which sits upon the capstone. This may not be as comic as it seems, for rabbits and hares were popularly reputed to be used as familiars by witches, servants of the Devil, and some form of witchcraft does seem to have been practised here at least in recent years. Once a dead hare was found lying beneath the huge stones, while on another occasion, feathers of wild birds were found scattered all around, and a piece of cardboard, protected by polythene and bearing strange symbols, was tied to one of the stones. While such attentions by covens are possibily a modern initiative rather than a traditional practice, they have made a most suitable choice in this site where the folklore points to the Church's efforts to connect it with the Devil as the god of an older religion. Some remnants of a ceremony of making an offering here appear to exist in the tradition that water poured at midnight into the natural cup-like cavities in the capstone will be gone by morning, drunk by the Devil. Water may seem an unremarkable substance to offer at a holy place, but in earlier centuries the water supply was less reliable than nowadays. Water then, as now, was the vital element in deciding whether crops grew, and people lived; hence the worship of wells and springs, sources of life. In that sense, water was the most precious offering possible.

Chute Causeway, near the Wiltshire/Hampshire border, is a Roman road remarkable in that it is deliberately curved to follow the line of the downs. In an open field a few yards to the north of the causeway, overlooking Black Down and Hippingscombe, there used to lie a flat stone with strange wavy markings upon it, supposedly known as the **Kinwardstone** (SU/310554 area). J. E. Jackson claimed that the stone was "traditionally the stone of one Kinward" who held his Hundred court here in what is Kinwardstone Hundred. A stone may well have existed to serve as the moot for the Hundred, but Gray maintains that the name as attached to this particular stone seems to have been an invention of Canon Jackson's. Its name apart, the stone has attracted typical stone-lore. During Gray's excavations a shepherd said the stone was called the 'Devil's waistcoat';

while the wavy markings were explained by another rustic as being the entrails of a man. This informant went on to assert that the holes in the stone were made in order to attach ropes and so move the stone. The attempt in question failed because the horses dropped dead. Obviously this stone's influence was more baleful than most. However, it does not seem to be in its place any more; probably it has had to·be moved to make way for the combine harvesters to work. One wonders how many tractors were needed to tow it away.

In contrast to the stones mentioned above, there has been no problem in moving the three **sarsen stones at Kingston Deverill** (ST/846371). For many years they lay near the river where the old road crossed; then a former rector named Mr. Clerk moved them to the rectory garden near the north-east corner of the churchyard. A later rector, Mr. Moore, moved them to their present position in a field east of the church, where the two larger stones were set upright with the smaller as a capstone, later removed for reasons of safety to lie beside the two uprights. An octogenarian, Mr. Carpenter, of the Post Office, Kingston Deverill, helped with this last move, and told how in his childhood the 'old people' said that the stones had originally been brought down from the hill above the village. The hill is called 'King's Hill' or 'King's Court Hill', and a tradition said that when on the hill the stones had been the meeting-place of kings. Fines had to be paid there, and executions were carried out. One suspects that this folklore stems partially from locals taking 'Kingston' to mean 'King's stone', when in fact it derives from old English 'cyninges tun', meaning 'the King's enclosure of land'. However, one can never rule out the possibility of a grain of truth in such tales. The great stones would serve admirably as a rallying-point where local grievances could be aired and punishments doled out. We have already seen how long Swanborough Tump remained in use as such a meeting-place.

A great sarsen stone which stands in Alton Barnes parish is called the **Hanging Stone** (SU/099605), and the field in which it is found is known as Hanging Stone Hurst. Local tradition explains how the stone got its name: a man who had stolen a sheep was carrying it away, supporting it by a rope slung round his neck. Reaching the great sarsen stone, he stopped to rest, putting the sheep on the stone; whereupon it slipped off on the side opposite to the one on which he was standing, and the rope tightened around the man's neck, so 'hanging' him. Obviously this far-fetched story is designed to fit the stone's title, yet the essential details are probably based on fact. The tale may recall the time when the penalty for sheep-stealing was hanging. The place of public hanging was often at a boundary stone of a parish or Hundred, and this hanging stone is only 100 yards from the parish boundary. It is notable that the sarsens at Kingston Deverill were also reputed to be the site of executions.

Avebury henge and stone circle (SU/003700), one of the largest ceremonial monuments in Europe, has stood since Neolithic times in relative obscurity on the Marlborough Downs. Its purpose must remain unknown in detail, but that it was a temple seems clear enough, both from the form of the Avebury complex, with the two great ceremonial avenues leading from the lesser circles at Beckhampton and Overton Hill, and from the diligence with which the Church sought to fell the stones in the Middle Ages. Indeed the efforts to obliterate this pagan site form the central theme of the folklore of Avebury.

Perhaps the most bewildering aspect of the folklore is how little there is of it: most marked is the lack of any legend to explain how the stones came there, as is found at circles like Stanton Drew and Stonehenge. It could be that this lack stems from the position of the village about and within the circle. Familiarity breeds contempt, and stones which have formed the background of village life, and which the villagers had broken up and used for building material, must necessarily be devoid of much of the mystery surrounding less mutilated circles standing in wild and lonely places. Moreover, Avebury has been a monument locally rather than nationally renowned. It escaped the attentions of mediaeval chroniclers, and John Aubrey was the first effectively to realise its archaeological significance and to attempt to detail and map its structure. Even today many people are unaware of its existence.

It may be, too, that the efforts of the early Church to wipe out the site have contributed to its obscurity. The mediaeval churchmen were obviously troubled by the pagan monument, and built a church deliberately at the site, but not within the circle: possibly even they feared to affront the former gods of the place too greatly. Instead they set about undermining its influence by felling the stones, a practice which reached its height in the fourteenth century. Even then it seems that the people feared to destroy the stones; instead, they were toppled over and buried in pits carefully dug to receive them. In this way God's work was done without upsetting the Devil too greatly. In the 1930s, Alexander Keiller, assisted by Stuart Piggott, excavated Avebury and re-erected those stones which were buried. Beneath one was found the skeleton of a man whose purse held the scissors and probe of a barber-surgeon, and coins dating from the fourteenth century. Aubrey Burl suggests that the crushing of the barber-surgeon may have temporarily stopped the destruction, for the people would have seen it as the stone's revenge on one who was foolhardy enough to attack them.[3]

[3] A. Burl, *Prehistoric Avebury*, (London, 1979), p. 36.

Yet in the seventeenth century, Aubrey was able to record that the stones were being felled once again, and this time without the former reverence, since they were valued as building material, and so broken up. "The manner is thus: they make a fire on that line of the stone where they would have it to crack; and after the stone is well heated, draw a line with cold water, and immediately give a smart knock with a smyth's sledge, and it will break like the collets at the glasse-house." The destruction went on in the eighteenth century, noted by Stukeley who worked with bitter industry to make his plans and notes before the monument should be totally destroyed. So it is that the Avebury we see today is a pale ghost of its former glory. There are reckoned to have been at least 180 great stones within the henge, and possibly 400 more in the avenues leading to it, most of which have been broken up. It is perhaps fitting that the monument of which so little remains should keep only a few scraps of folklore.

There is apparently a general belief that snakes cannot live within the circle. This belief may tie in with the pagan element, in that a symbol of the Devil is the serpent. While one might therefore expect that snakes would be believed to flourish rather than to die in a pagan place, a carving on the twelfth-century church font may shed a little light on this tradition. It shows a bishop with his crozier crushing the head of a serpent-like beast: the Church defeating the Devil and destroying his power. (Fig. 4)

Font carving, Avebury church.

In a sense, this is an accurate picture of the situation at Avebury. The Church began the work of destroying the Devil's temple, and the symbols of the Evil One's power are broken. Still some relics of his influence remain in the names of some of the stones. The Beckhampton Cove, which stood at the end of the western avenue, was known in the eighteenth century as the Devil's Quoits (SU/089694), while the Cove within the north inner circle was called the Devil's Brand Irons. The huge stone at the south entrance is still called the Devil's Chair. Not surprisingly, when one of the Devil's Quoits was broken up c. 1720, the two stones remaining became known by the more Christian – or at least, Old Testament – names of Adam and Eve.

Avebury - part of the circle in early morning mist.

The West Kennet avenue leading to Avebury.

Avebury - stone at the south entrance.

Stonehenge by Edgar Barclay after Inigo Jones.

One of the most striking of Avebury's stones is the great Diamond Stone, also called the Swindon Stone because it stands beside the road to Swindon. It is said to cross the road when it hears the church clock strike midnight. This is a typical piece of stone-lore, with many similar examples in other parts of the country. The Long Stone at Minchinhampton, Gloucestershire, runs around the field when the clock strikes twelve; and the Tingle Stone at the long barrow at Avening, Gloucestershire, also runs, around the field when it hears the clock strike midnight. These tales can be taken in one of two ways. On the one hand, the insistence on movement and hearing in the stones stresses the life in them; but on the other hand, the sceptical will say that as stones cannot possibly hear, they will never hear the clock strike and so will never be seen moving. Both believers and sceptics can thus be satisfied by the same tale.

Finally, it remains briefly to mention some of Avebury circle's ghosts, possibly the most ancient phantoms in the country. Kathleen Wiltshire records how small figures were seen moving among the stones one bright January night. Miss Dunn who claimed to have seen the figures described "a most uncanny feeling", as if she were seeing Ancient Britons engaged upon some ceremonial of long ago.

Stonehenge (SU/123422) alone of Wiltshire's ancient monuments will certainly need no introduction to the reader. It has been well known for many centuries; and throughout documented history, stories and speculation about its origin and purpose have been rife. The traditions fall into two more or less distinct types: the writings of early scholars, and the oral traditions of the local people. Since the oral traditions would seem to derive in part from the written, both must be taken into account. As the legends and folklore of Stonehenge have already been discussed in great detail in a work by Grinsell[4], only Geoffrey of Monmouth's seminal scholarly account, and the traditions reckoned to be 'of the folk' will be considered here.

Geoffrey of Monmouth, writing c. 1136, tells how the great stones came to be set up on Salisbury Plain. King Aurelius Ambrosius, brother of Uther Pendragon the father of King Arthur, wanted a monument suitable to honour the memory of three hundred of his men who had died in battle. It was the enchanter Merlin who suggested: "If thou be fain to grace the burial-place of these men with a work that shall endure for ever, send for the Dance of the Giants that is in Killare, a mountain in Ireland ... and so they be set up round this plot in a circle, even as they be now there set up, here shall they stand for ever."

[4] L. V. Grinsell, *The legendary history and folklore of Stonehenge*, (St. Peter Port, Guernsey, 1975).

Aurelius was so fain, and sent his brother Uther, with Merlin and an army, to defeat the Irish and bring away the stones. The Irish were duly defeated, but nobody could take down the stones, until Merlin "put together his own engines" and "laid the stones down so lightly as none would believe". The Dance was taken to Britain by ship and reconstructed in the place where it stands today. Perhaps the most remarkable part of this narrative is Merlin the Enchanter's use of 'engines' rather than magic in dismantling the circle: surely this part of the narrative contains a shadow of the truth.

The name 'Dance of the Giants' may point to some legend that the stones were people or giants turned to stone. Such legends are common enough at stone circles: the Rollright Stones are a king and his knights turned to stone by a witch; while the Stanton Drew circle is a wedding party turned to stone by the Devil as a result of having danced on a Sunday. S. P. Menefee suspects that 'Giants' Dance' actually refers to the size of the stones and their circular form, but he also cites L. Spence who gives the version that the stones were giants petrified for their impieties. Many variations on the theme are possible, and it is certain that such a legend would have grown and taken different forms before dying out.

It is interesting that Geoffrey of Monmouth stresses the virtues and healing qualities of the stones. "For in these stones is a mystery, and a healing virtue against many ailments ... they did wash the stones and pour forth the water into baths, whereby they that were sick were made whole. Moreover, they did mix confections of herbs with the water, whereby they that were wounded had healing, for not a stone is there that lacketh in virtue of leechcraft." Healing is a power especially associated with many stones, and the means of gaining a cure varies from simply touching the stone to crawling through a hole in it. The process Geoffrey notes is comparatively involved.

Some 600 years after Geoffrey's time, a man known as Gaffer Hunt had a hut built against one of the great upright stones, and here he kept liquor with which to regale visitors after he had shown them the stones. It is to old Gaffer Hunt that the folk version of the stones' origin and the more widely-known story of the Friar's Heel, have been tentatively ascribed. J. Wood records the tale, which tells how Merlin employed the Devil to get the stones from "a backside belonging to an old woman in Ireland". The Devil, disguised as a gentleman, showed the woman a bag of money and offered her as much as she could count while he took away the stones. The woman agreed, but had hardly touched the first coin when the stones disappeared by magic. Thus she was tricked out of possession of both the stones and the money. The Devil carried the stones back to Salisbury Plain, dropping one into the river Avon at Bulford on the way, and set them up, boasting as he completed the task that none should ever know how they came there. However, a friar who had witnessed the full reconstruction could not help calling out "that is more than thee canst tell", before making off towards safer ground. The Devil lobbed a stone after him which hit him upon the heel, and the mark of the Friar's heel remains on the Heel Stone to this day. This tale shows how by this time the Devil had come to be associated with ancient pagan sites and magical feats demanding demonic powers, for Merlin makes only the briefest of appearances before the Devil takes over. The incident shows the Church getting the better – more or less – of an encounter with the Evil One once again. Heavey maintains that the Heel Stone is so called because it leans or heels over, and that the legend has been created around the name, making of it a good moral tale in the process.[5] It is interesting how the reference to the dropped stone ties in with the tradition already noted about the stone at Bulford.

A tradition that the stones could not be counted alike twice running dates at least from the sixteenth century, when Sir Philip Sidney referred to it in his sonnet 'The seven wonders of England' (1598). Charles II, fleeing after his defeat at Worcester in 1651, found time to count the stones correctly twice over, but the tradition persisted. Charles Dickens records the nineteenth-century version: "no one could count the stones of Stonehenge twice, and make the same number of them, likewise ... anyone who counted them three times nine times, and then stood in the centre and said 'I dare!' would behold a tremendous apparition, and be stricken dead". Several strands of folklore are woven together here: the dislike of things supernatural of being counted, for fear of the power gained over them by that means; the mystic power of three and multiples of three; and the punishment which would fall on those daring to try to gain ascendancy over sacred and ancient powers.

Defoe first notes the variant of the 'baker and the loaves', or how a baker thought to count the stones by putting a loaf on every one, yet still could not arrive at the same answer twice running. Similar tales are told of other sites, like the Countless Stones in Kent, where the Devil ate one of the loaves and so ensured the total would be wrong. It may be that in this curious tale remains the distant memory of offerings made to the stones and perhaps accepted on their behalf by a priest of the cult.

The tales told of Stonehenge are clearly a mixture of a little folklore common to many such sites and much embroidery specific to the great circle

---

[5] J. F. Heavey, 'The Heele Stone', *Folklore* 88, (1977), pp. 238 – 9.

in particular. It is almost impossible to separate the 'genuine' lore from the literary embellishments of specific individuals. Yet ultimately, the legends of Stonehenge and of other Wiltshire stones conform to the recognised folklore themes, in some of which it seems we may yet catch some glimpse, albeit corrupted by time and people's changing attitudes, of the ways of our distant forbears.

"... and the trees and the grass do not now remember them. Only I hear the stones lament them: 'deep they delved us, fair they wrought us, high they builded us; but they are gone'."[6]

---

[6] J. R. R. Tolkien, *The Fellowship of the Ring*, 2nd ed., (London, 1966), p. 297.

AFTERWORD

One might be pardoned for thinking that in our modern scientific world there is no place for folklore with its bizarre tales and superstitions. It seems that the old beliefs and legends have long been thought to be dying out. John Aubrey in the seventeenth century feared that the Civil War had made the old traditions lose their vitality, while eighteenth-century reason and nineteenth-century materialism were also supposed to have routed superstition. Yet the records of Victorian folklorists showed that the country traditions were as strong as ever; while among the wealthy, spiritualism was flourishing. In our own time there is much evidence for the survivial of 'irrational' beliefs, both in the occult and in folklore. Horoscopes and forms of fortune-telling are widely popular, while many people consult mediums and clairvoyants. Magic – black, white, and shades of grey – is still practised, covertly or overtly. Occasionally these practices come to the attention of the general public when evidence of magical activities is found, like the witch-card which was tied to the Devil's Den near Marlborough. It seems that in areas where science fails them, people turn to the occult for enlightment.

As for folklore itself, while many of the old traditions, like throwing coins into wells, still continue, new ones which reflect modern preoccupations are also arising. Where once mankind feasted the imagination on tales of gods and monsters coming from wild and lonely places on Earth, we now look for mystery to the stars and the infinite possibilities of the universe. Popular literature, cinema and television all reflect this preoccupation, and folklore is no exception.

The county of Wiltshire, being essentially rural, has retained its consciousness of the past rather more than other less rural counties, so that the changeover to modern forms of folklore and 'urban legend' is slow to take place. Yet the signs of changeover are there, nevertheless. Today the old gods and dragons which haunted the downs have been usurped by Unidentified Flying Objects which, it is claimed, orient themselves on ancient sites and hill figures, such as Cley Hill and the Westbury white horse near Warminster, a prime area for UFO-spotting. For some years now, the media have reported strange circles and formations which appear mysteriously in cornfields in the Warminster area. Popular opinion ascribes them to the actions of UFOs. Meanwhile, as we have seen at Oliver's Castle near Devizes, people use metal-detectors in their search for buried treasure in hill-forts. Phantom coaches and horses are replaced by spectral cars and aircraft: a ghostly World War I aeroplane has several times been seen crashing to destruction over Salisbury Plain. The car itself has gathered its own brand of folklore. Pieces of chain or rubber trailing from back bumpers are there as a cure for nausea: the chain touching the road is supposed to disperse the static electricity which 'causes' car-sickness. Apparently folklore is acquiring a pseudo-scientific element.

The paradox of folklore is that, though dismissed as 'what the old folk believe', it does not die with those old believers. Each generation embellishes what has gone before and adds new traditions to the existing ones. It seems that mankind craves an element of mystery on which to exercise its imagination, and while there remains one aspect of life to be explained or one corner of the universe yet to be explored, lore and legend will flourish.

INDEX

COMPREHENSIVE BIBLIOGRAPHY

Abbreviation

WAM   *Wiltshire Archaeological and Natural History Magazine*

Bibliography

G.W.G. Allen and A. D. Passmore, 'Earthen circles near Highworth' *WAM* 47 (1935-7), 114-22

The Anglo-Saxon Chronicle (London, 1953)

Anon., 'Hanging stone' *WAM* 42 (1922-4), 75

G. Ashe, *King Arthur's Avalon: the story of Glastonbury* (Glasgow, 1973)

J. Aubrey, *Monumenta Britannica*, ed. J. Fowles (Sherborne, 1980)

J. Aubrey, *Natural history of Wiltshire* (New York, 1969)

M. Baker, *Folklore and customs of rural England* (Newton Abbot, 1974)

Bede, T*he ecclesiastical history of the English nation*, trans. J. Stevens (London, 1910)

J. and C. Bord, *Mysterious Britain* (London, 1974)

J. and C. Bord, *The secret country* (London, 1978)

A. G. Bradley, *Round about Wiltshire* 3rd ed. (London, 1913)

B. Branston, *The lost gods of England* (London, 1974)

H. C. Brentall, 'Marlborough Castle' *WAM* 48 (1937-9), 133-43

K. M. Briggs, *A dictionary of fairies, hobgoblins, brownies, bogies and other supernatural creatures* (Harmondsworth, 1977)

K. M. Briggs, 'The fairies and the realms of the dead' *Folklore* 81 (1970), 81-96

T. Brown, 'The black dog' *Folklore* 69 (1958), 175-92

J. H. Brunvand, *The vanishing hitchhiker: American urban legends and their meanings* (London, 1983)

A. Burl, *Prehistoric Avebury* (London, 1979)

J. E. Chandler, *A history of Marlborough: the gateway to Ancient Britain* (Marlborough, 1977)

R. Coward, 'Roundway Hill' *Devizes Gazette*, May 16, 1985

K. Crossley-Holland, *The Norse Myths* (Harmondsworth, 1980)

T. S. Cunningham, 'Marden' *Wiltshire Notes and Queries* 7 (1911-3), 388-93

B. H. Cunnington, 'The Manton barrow legend' *WAM* 50 (1942-4), 483-4

B. H. and M. E. Cunnington, 'Casterley Camp' *WAM* 38 (1913-4), 53-105

M. E. Cunnington, 'Figsbury Rings' WAM 43 (1925-7), 48-58

M. E. Cunnington, A*n introduction to the archaeology of Wiltshire, from the earliest times to the pagan Saxons* (Devizes, 1933)

M. E. Cunnington, 'Knap Hill Camp' *WAM* 37 (1911-2)

M. E. Cunnington, 'List of the long barrows of Wiltshire' *WAM* 38 (1913-4), 379-414

M. E. Cunnington, 'The re-erection of two fallent stones, and discovery of an interment with a drinking cup, at Avebury' *WAM* 38 (1913-4), 1-11

M.E. Cunnington, Sarsen stones at Kingston Deverill' *WAM* 44 (1927-9), 261-2

W. Cunnington, 'Barrows on Roundway Hill' *WAM* 22 (1884-5), 340-1

C. Dickens, *The Holly-tree* (London, 1855)

Domesday book, v. 6 Wiltshire, ed. C. and F. Thorn (Chichester, 1979)

A. Dryden, *Memorials of old Wiltshire* (London, 1906)

E. Ekblom, *The place-names of Wiltshire: their origin and history* (Uppsala, 1917)

H. R. Ellis Davidson, 'Folklore and history' *Folklore* 85 (1974), 73-92

H. R. Ellis Davidson, 'Folklore and man's past' *Folklore* 73-4 (1962-3), 527-44

J. P. Emslie, 'Scraps of folklore' *Folklore* 26 (1915), 168

Encyclopaedia of world mythology (London, 1975)

G. E. Evans, *The pattern under the plough: aspects of the folk-life of East Anglia* (London, 1966)

N. Fairbairn, *A traveller's guide to the kingdoms of Arthur* (London, 1983)

A. Fraser, *Cromwell: our chief of men* (London, 1973)

M. Gelling, *Signposts to the past: place-names and the history of England* (London, 1978)

Geoffrey of Monmouth, *History of the Kings of Britain*, trans. S. Evans (London, 1958)

C. V. Goddard, 'Wiltshire folk lore jottings' *WAM* 50 (1942-4), 24-46

E. H. Goddard, *Wiltshire bibliography* (Frome, Wiltshire, 1929)

J. E. B. Gover, *The place-names of Wiltshire* (Cambridge, 1939)

H. St. G. Gray, The so-called "Kenward Stone" at Chute Causeway, Wilts.' *WAM* 43 (1925-7), 207-12

G. Grigson, *Geoffrey Grigson's countryside: the classic companion to rural Britain* (London, 1982)

L. V. Grinsell, 'Barrow treasure, in fact, tradition, and legislation' *Folklore* 78 (1967), 1-38

L. V. Grinsell, *Folklore of Prehistoric sites in Britain* (Newton Abbot, 1976)

L. V. Grinsell, *Legendary history and folklore of Stonehenge* (St. Peter Port, Guernsey, 1975)

L. V. Grinsell, 'Notes on the folklore of Prehistoric sites in Britain' *Folklore* 90 (1979), 66-70

L. V. Grinsell, 'Scheme for recording the folklore of Prehistoric remains' *Folklore* 50 (1939), 323-32

G. B. Grundy, 'The place-names of Wiltshire' *WAM* 41 (1920-2), 335-53

H. A. Guerber, *The myths of Greece and Rome: their stories, signification and origin* (London, 1911)

C. Harvey, *The ancient temple at Avebury and its gods* (London, 1923)

R. M. Heaney, 'Silbury Hill' *Folklore* 24 (1913), 524

J. F. Heavey, 'The Heele stone' *Folklore* 88 (1977), 238-9

Historical atlas of Britain (London, 1981)

R. C. Hoare, T*he ancient history of north Wiltshire* (London, 1821)

R. C. Hoare, *The ancient history of south Wiltshire* (London, 1812)

C. Hole, *A dictionary of British folk customs* (London, 1978)

D. Ibberson, *Two Wiltshire villages: an approach to the history of Oare with Rainscombe, and Huish* (Marlborough, 1963)

J. E. Jackson, 'Notes on the border of Wilts and Hants' *WAM* 21 (1882-3), 330-54

J. E. Jackson 'The vale of Warminster' *WAM* 17 (1878), 282-306

K. H. Jackson, *A Celtic miscellany* (Aylesbury, 1971)

E. G. H. Kempson, *Marlborough College: a short history and guide* (Brentwood, 1979)

L. Laing, *Celtic Britain* (London, 1981)

L. and J. Laing, *Anglo-Saxon England* (London, 1982)

L. and J. Laing, *The origins of Britain* (London, 1982)

J. A. Leete, *Wiltshire miscellany* (Melksham, 1976)

A. MacKenzie, *Apparitions and ghosts: a modern study* (London, 1971)

The Mabinogion, trans J. Gantz (Harmondsworth, 1977)

M. Marples, *White horses and other hill figures* (Gloucester, 1981)

A. S. Mellor, 'Excavation of a circular mound on Totney Hill, Kingsdown, Box, Aug. 1934' *WAM* 47 (1935-7), 169-76

S. P. Menefee, 'The "Countless Stones": a final reckoning' *Folklore* 86 (1975), 146-66

S. P. Menefee, 'The "Merry Maidens" and the "Noce de Pierre"' *Folklore* 85 (1974), 23-42

J. Merewether, *Diary of a dean* (London, 1851)

C. Millson, *Tales of old Wiltshire* (Newbury, 1982)

E. Olivier, *Moonrakings: a little book of Wiltshire stories* (Warminster, 1979)

G. Osborn, *Exploring ancient Wiltshire* (Sherborne, 1982)

J. B. Partridge, 'Wiltshire folklore' *Folklore* 26 (1915), 211-12

A. D. Passmore, 'Fieldwork in N. Wilts 1926-28: (Barrow Chisledon 2)' *WAM* 44 (1927-9), 241

C. Phythian-Adams, *Local history and folklore: a new framework* (London, 1975)

S. Piggott, *The West Kennet long barrow* (London, 1962)

J. U. Powell, 'Folklore notes from south-west Wilts.' *Folklore* 12 (1901) 71-83

Reader's Digest Associaion, *Folklore, myths and legends of Britain* 2nd ed. (London, 1977)

J. B. Russell, *Witchcraft in the middle ages* (London, 1972)

J. S. Ryan, 'Othin in England' *Folklore* 73-4 (1962-3), 460-80

G. H. Skipworth, 'Folklore jottings from the western counties' *Folklore* 5 (1894), 339-40

A. Smith, 'The image of Cromwell in folklore and tradition' *Folklore* 79 (1968), 17-39

A. C. Smith, 'Silbury' *WAM* 7 (1860-1), 145-91

L. Spence, *Minor traditions of British mythology* (London, 1941)

E. H. Stone, *The stones of Stonehenge* (London, 1924)

T. Story-Maskelyne, <u>note</u> in *Wiltshire Notes and Queries* 6 (1908-10), 45

T. Story-Maskelyne, 'Tan Hill Fair' *WAM* 34 (1905-6), 426-32

W. Stukeley, *Abury: a temple of the British Druids* (London, 1743)

W. Stukeley, *Stonehenge: a temple restor'd to the British Druids* (London, 1740)

C. Thomas, 'Folklore from a Wiltshire village' *Folklore* 65-6 (1954-5), 165-8

K. Thomas, *Religion and the decline of magic: studies in popular belief in 16th and 17th century England* (London, 1971)

N. Thomas, *A guide to Prehistoric England* 2nd ed. (London, 1976)

J. Thurnam, 'Barrows on the downs of North Wiltshire' *WAM* 6 (1859-60), 317-36

J. Thurnam, 'On the barrow at Lanhill nr. Chippenham' *WAM* 3 (1855-7), 67-86

H. W. Timperley, *The Vale of Pewsey* (London, 1954)

J. R. R. Tolkien, *The Fellowship of the Ring* 2nd ed. (London, 1966)

P. Underwood, *Dictionary of the occult and supernatural: an A to Z of hauntings, possession, witchcraft, demonology and other occult phenomena* (Glasgow, 1979)

P. Underwood, *Ghosts of Wales* (London, 1978)

The Victoria history of the counties of England: a history of Wiltshire (London, 1957)

E. Waring, *Ghosts and legends of the Dorset countryside* (Tisbury, Wiltshire, 1977)

R. Whitlock, *The folklore of Wiltshire* (London, 1976)

R. Whitlock, *In search of lost gods: a guide to British folklore* (Oxford, 1979)

R. Whitlock, *Wiltshire* (London, 1976)

J. P. Williams-Freeman, *Field archaeology as illustrated by Hampshire* (London, 1915)

'Wiltoniensis', Swanborough Ashes' *Wiltshire Notes and Queries* 2 (1896-8), 243-5

K. Wiltshire, *Ghosts and legends of the Wiltshire countryside* (Salisbury, 1973)

K. Wiltshire, *Wiltshire folklore* (Salisbury, 1975)

J. Wood, *Choir Gaure* (Oxford, 1747)

M. Wood, *In search of the Dark Ages* (London, 1981)